With love,
June x

Good Taste

# JANE GREEN

Good Taste

SIMPLE, DELICIOUS RECIPES
FOR FAMILY AND FRIENDS

PHOTOGRAPHY BY TOM McGOVERN

NEW AMERICAN LIBRARY
*New York*

NEW AMERICAN LIBRARY
Published by Berkley
An imprint of Penguin Random House LLC
375 Hudson Street, New York, New York 10014

GOOD TASTE: SIMPLE DELICIOUS RECIPES FOR FAMILY AND FRIENDS

ISBN: 9780399583377

Collector's edition, 2015
Berkley hardcover edition, October 2016

Printed in the United States of America
1   3   5   7   9   10   8   6   4   2

Cover and book design by Russ Hardin and Carol Buettner
Interior photographs by Tom McGovern
Interior illustrations by Jane Green

FOR MY LATE GRANDMA, AND MY MUM

Who taught me that food is love

# CONTENTS

∽

# FROM JANE

This is not a book about food. This is a book about gathering family and friends in a warm, comfortable, welcoming kitchen and feeding them the kinds of food that make them feel loved.

I grew up with a mother who cooked, who collected recipes in a file or scrawled them down, ingredients only, never quantities, able to retain the rest in her head. I would perch on a kitchen stool as she baked, taking the pastry scraps and rolling them out for jam tarts, making peppermint creams for the school sale.

When I was at university, I would come home during vacations, often to an empty house with my parents away at our house in France. I would proceed to invite all my friends over, cooking elaborate meals, stratas and quiches for brunches, delicious desserts. I was a bold and fearless cook, never afraid to try something new, moving swiftly on when it didn't work out.

There were, inevitably, disasters. I hoped to impress a new boyfriend by cooking a Thai green curry for his closest friends. The recipe called for four large green peppers. My local grocery store only carried tiny green peppers, so I bought 16 of them, figuring that might make up the difference, not realizing each tiny one packed more heat than an Exocet missile. I almost set everyone's mouth on fire, but happily it was great material for a scene in one of my early books, *Jemima J*, in which Jemima fails miserably at impressing her prospective future in-laws.

For years, when people asked me if I loved to cook, I nodded, because as far back as I can remember, there was nothing I loved more than gathering people together in the kitchen and feeding them.

Then I had children. Suddenly I had no time and everyone needed to be fed, every day. I no longer had the luxury of spending the day chopping and dicing, and it all started to feel like far more of a burden than a pleasure.

I started looking for different kinds of recipes, ones that didn't require sautéing for hours, ones that didn't keep me enslaved to the stove. I wanted recipes that were quick and easy, that could be thrown together without much thought, that I could give to the children and just as easily serve at a dinner party. My two requirements were ease and an impressive, and (naturally) delicious, result.

I quickly realized that for me, having people over is less about the food, and more about comfort, warmth, nurture. It is about creating the kind of welcoming environment that instantly makes people feel relaxed and cared for, that truly brings meaning to the concept of food being love.

With the children came the tuna casserole years. I shall spare you the recipe, although one of my babysitters from those years still swears by it and makes it for her own children today. There was much meatloaf and many meatballs. And it all felt dull. I always cooked from scratch though, and we always sat together as a family. We still do. My children may be running off to basketball, or rowing or out with friends, but most days of the week everyone comes home to sit around the large old table in our kitchen to eat home-cooked food.

I discovered that everyday cooking doesn't interest me nearly as much as entertaining does. I am not as sociable as people might expect, and would much rather be at home than anywhere else. My perfect evening always involves gathering the people I love in my kitchen, filling square glass vases with peonies and lavender from the garden, lining the table with creamy pillar candles of different heights and cooking for everyone there.

We have a dining room, but I would rather have crystal glasses on the table in the kitchen, be able to jump up and grab things, dress salads in full view so I don't miss a moment of conversation.

The setting may be beautiful thanks to the flowers and candles, the light glistening off crystal glasses, but it is always informal. Friends help chop the salad as I brown the onions. Bottles of wine are poured by whoever's around, and spiced nuts scooped out of bowls as people perch on the stools around the island.

I'm not a huge believer in hors d'oeuvres. Perhaps it is because I was brought up in England, without the kind of abundance around food that exists in the United States. I have been to too many parties this side of the pond with such delicious and copious hors d'oeuvres that by the time dinner is served, everyone is full.

I would rather put out nuts, a cheese platter and some fresh fruit—grapes or figs for the cheese—so that by the time people come to the table, they are hungry, and the food will taste that much better.

I have had a little training—a few weeks at the French Culinary Institute in New York—but the recipes here are ones I have lovingly collected, in some cases adapted and in a few, created, over the years. Occasionally, a recipe is so perfect it needs nothing other than attribution. I have done my best to credit those who put the work and effort into creating their own wonderful dishes so that they appear exactly as they intended, and I have attempted to track down those that I found online.

So not all this food is mine. But it is what I cook and what I love. Whatever its provenance, the food contained within these pages has a strong leaning toward my childhood in England and is both delicious and easy. It makes you feel nurtured, comforted and loved.

And what, after all, is better on a cold winter's day than being nurtured, comforted and loved?

With love,

June x.

# Beginnings...

All summer long I serve salads as a starter, but as soon as the weather gets cold I start craving hot food. Soups, roasted vegetables and tarts with buttery, melting pastry.

My favorite thing of all is to serve the soup in mugs while we're by the fire in the living room. We have friends who have a very old farmhouse with an enormous fireplace, and they regularly hold fireside dinners, all of us sitting around the fire as they bring out an assortment of antique contraptions on which to cook dinner. It is always delicious, and there is something so cozy about eating by a fire with friends. We can't cook meals in the little old fireplace in our house, much as I would like to, but going from the fire to a table on which sit delicious tarts, red wine and crusty bread is almost, almost as nice.

# SPINACH AND GRUYÈRE CRUSTLESS TART

This actually doubles as a great lunch dish served with a salad, almost like a crustless quiche. Speaking of crusts, we are tending toward low-carbohydrate foods these days, and this always feels like a spectacularly healthy alternative to quiche. I'm lucky in that the one vegetable all my kids adore is spinach, and spinach with cream and cheese? That's like getting to heaven early.

SERVES 6–8

## Ingredients:

Butter for baking dish

3 packages frozen chopped spinach, thawed and squeezed dry

1½ cups half-and-half

3 large eggs, beaten

1½ cups grated gruyère cheese

2 teaspoons salt

⅛ teaspoon pepper

¼ teaspoon ground nutmeg

## Method:

Preheat oven to 350 degrees.

Butter a shallow baking dish.

In a bowl combine spinach, half-and-half, eggs, 1 cup cheese, salt, pepper and nutmeg.

Stir and spread in baking dish, and top with remaining gruyère.

Bake until set and top is golden brown, 30–35 minutes.

# EGGPLANT, MOZZARELLA AND ROSEMARY SLICES

Years ago, when I first moved to the United States, I noticed something peculiar about entertaining. Every time I invited someone for lunch or dinner or a barbeque, they brought food with them. I was, at the time, utterly bewildered.

"Do they think I can't cook?" I would whisper to my then-husband, as I placed their apple pie on the counter, wondering what I should do with the chocolate mousse I had slaved over all afternoon.

In England I was used to bringing things to dinner parties, but not food for the actual party itself. Flowers, wine or chocolates, which were likely to be brought out as an after-dinner treat. Here I was, in America, inundated with food that wasn't on my menu. One weekend I cooked an Indian feast, and my guests arrived with platters of shrimp cocktail and chicken wings.

Looking back, I realize that when I first moved here, I was still learning how to be a grown-up. I was newly married, a youngish mother, doing the things I thought newly married youngish mothers were supposed to do, which included throwing dinner parties. I was doing the things my mother did, not realizing that we are no longer living in the age of *Mad Men* and it really isn't necessary to seat guests awkwardly around beautifully laid tables in formal dining rooms, serving them fine French food in order for the evening to be deemed a success.

Ten years on, I no longer have formal dinner parties. Ever. I will set the table beautifully, but in the kitchen or on the terrace. I love my guests bringing food, and more, love when they grab a knife and start chopping vegetables for the salad.

Entertaining, for me, is all about comfort and ease. It is about creating a beautiful environment, but one in which my guests will instantly feel at home. Nothing makes me happier than people kicking off their shoes and curling up on one of the sofas with a big glass of wine moments after they've arrived.

And I love them bringing food. If I am preparing something special—a Thai meal or Middle Eastern—I will request they bring nothing, or perhaps just hors d'oeuvres, but these days I am enormously grateful to anyone who eases the burden of everything life throws at us.

These eggplant slices are about the least burdensome starter I can think of, with the cheese and herb oil transporting the dish to a whole other level. It works equally well without dredging in egg and bread crumbs, just grilling the eggplant to a tender sweetness, which is what, in these low-carb times, I so often do. I think the bread-free version is Nigel Slater's.

# EGGPLANT, MOZZARELLA AND ROSEMARY SLICES

SERVES 4–6

## Ingredients:

**1 large eggplant**

**2 eggs, beaten**

**¾ cup bread crumbs**

**4 sprigs rosemary, woody stems discarded**

**¼ cup olive oil**

**1 ball of mozzarella**

**¼ cup pine kernels, toasted**

**Salt and pepper**

## Method:

Preheat oven to 350 degrees.

Slice the eggplant into rounds, about ½" thick. Dip in egg then dredge in bread crumbs until completely coated. Bake for 15–20 minutes until golden and tender.

With a hand blender, blend the olive oil and rosemary until thoroughly mixed.

Thinly slice mozzarella and place a slice on each piece of eggplant, putting back into oven until cheese is melted with golden spots.

Drizzle with remaining oil, season with salt and pepper, and scatter pine kernels over to serve.

# POTATO, GORGONZOLA AND SAGE BREAD

I love baking bread. When I lived—very briefly—on Middleduck Farm in the heart of the countryside in Connecticut's Litchfield Hills, I instantly became Mrs. Walton, making jam and baking bread every day. There is nothing like the smell of fresh-baked bread, and somehow living in the middle of nowhere on a very old farm with a leaky roof, I felt it would have been, well, *bad form*, really, not to have baked bread.

I baked bread all day. Eggy bread, brioche, whole wheat bread, scones. Sometimes, it turned out beautifully, sometimes it was an unleavened heap. I always breathed a sigh of relief when it came out well, a bit like, I imagine, winning at Russian roulette.

Unlike serious bread bakers, I still have no idea how it *works*. I know about making a *starter*, and letting it *prove* (rise) before punching it down, etc., etc., but I don't really *understand* it. I do quite like experimenting with bread—adding caramelized onions, honey, maple syrup, nuts— and am perfectly happy to chuck it out when it doesn't work. Which clearly, I had to do with all the unleavened heaps.

I had tried to make this bread before, but the recipe didn't have yeast in it. Unsurprisingly, the bread was flat and heavy. Bread with potato tends to be stickier anyway, so this time I added 2 teaspoons of dried yeast, fermented in ¼ cup warm water for 15–20 minutes until bubbly and yeasty-smelling. I know, I know, I didn't know what yeasty-smelling meant either, but once you smell it, you won't forget it. It's sour and . . . well . . . *yeasty*.

With the addition of the yeast, the bread came out perfectly. Even better toasted, I should imagine, with dollops of leftover Bagna Càuda (page 12) on top . . . (I will not be finding out as I am now firmly back on the wagon, and bread is not invited on with me until extra poundage after that dinner has gone.)

# POTATO, GORGONZOLA AND SAGE BREAD

SERVES 8

## Ingredients:

2 teaspoons rapid-rise yeast

1⅓ cups mashed potatoes, either warm or cold

4½ cups all-purpose flour

1 tablespoon salt

1 tablespoon plain Greek yogurt

1⅓ cups warm water

½ cup crumbled gorgonzola cheese

Handful of fresh sage, finely chopped

## Method:

First get the starter going. Mix the yeast with ¼ cup of warm water and set aside for 15–20 minutes until it starts to bubble and rise.

Mix potatoes with 4 cups of flour, salt and yeast mixture in a stand mixer bowl. Add yogurt, then water, slowly. Using a dough hook, give it around 10 minutes. It will be very sticky, so turn it onto a well-floured surface and knead by hand, adding at least ½ cup of flour, until it is soft and elastic—around 5–10 minutes. This is my favorite bit, when I do truly feel like I am living on Walton mountain.

When done, turn out into a well-oiled bowl (just coat with olive oil), cover with a damp dishcloth and put in a cold place overnight, or a warm place for 1–2 hours.

When the dough is doubled in size, heat the oven to 425 degrees, punch the dough down, add the gorgonzola and sage and fold the dough over. Knead for a couple of minutes until cheese and herbs are evenly spread, then form into a round loaf. Set bread on a baking sheet, loosely covered with a damp dishcloth (keep the cloth damp or the dough will stick to it). After about half an hour the dough will be doubled in size.

Put the bread in the oven for 20 minutes, then turn the temperature down to 375 degrees, and cook for another 10 minutes or until it's cooked through. You can tell it's cooked by knocking on the loaf's underside—when it's cooked, it sounds hollow.

# BAGNA CÀUDA

This literally means "hot bath," and in Italy vegetables are dipped into it, then eaten with a slice of bread held underneath to catch the drippings.

Think salty fondue, and you'll get the picture. As a huge fan of anchovies (I am that rare person who always orders Caesar salad with extra anchovies), there is nothing better for me, and if you like salty food, I urge you to try it.

SERVES 6–8

### Ingredients:

¾ cup olive oil

6 tablespoons (¾ stick) unsalted butter, room temperature

12 anchovy fillets

6 large garlic cloves, chopped

Salt and pepper

Assorted fresh vegetables, cut into bite-size pieces

1 recipe Potato, Gorgonzola and Sage Bread (page 10), cut into pieces

### Method:

Blend oil, butter, anchovies and garlic in a food processor until smooth, then put in a medium-sized pan. Cook over low heat, stirring occasionally, for 15 minutes. Season with salt and pepper. Serve warm with vegetables and bread.

# PROSCIUTTO AND SAGE WRAPPED DATES

I know I said I wasn't a huge fan of hors d'oeuvres, but when the inclination does strike, this is what I make, and they have become something of a tradition at Christmas. They are what I can only classify as dangerous food.

I have a particular proclivity for food that is salty and sweet, and this is about as salty (from the prosciutto) and as sweet (from the dates and maple syrup) as it gets. The Japanese have a word, *umami*, which essentially means a pleasant savory taste, but there is no word as far as I know for the perfect combination of salty and sweet. Perhaps we ought to make one up. Either way, this is about as close to heaven as one can get with food.

Although I have said this will serve six, assuming everyone will eat two, experience has taught that this is far more likely to serve four. And occasionally one.

SERVES 4–6

### Ingredients:

24 fresh sage leaves

12 dates, halved, pits removed

1 pack prosciutto, each piece sliced lengthways down the middle

2 tablespoons maple syrup

### Method:

Preheat oven to 350 degrees.

Place a sage leaf on each date half, wrap with prosciutto and place flat side down on a baking sheet.

Bake 10 minutes. Brush with maple syrup and serve.

# SWEET AND SOUR NUTS

I once went to a dinner party where the hostess was a renowned cook. The party was called for 6:30 p.m., and we all showed up, very excited about what was bound to be a spectacular meal.

First, there were drinks. And a giant bowl of spiced nuts, which were the perfect combination of sweet and spicy and desperately moreish. The bowl happened to be just in front of me, and I sat on the sofa, nursing my cocktail, occasionally helping myself to just a few nuts.

An hour went by. I had a few more nuts. Two hours went by. Many more nuts disappeared into my mouth. At half past nine, the hostess jumped up in horror, not realizing the time. Well, thank *God*! I thought, starving.

"I'm so sorry!" she exclaimed, disappearing into the kitchen. "I'd better start cooking!"

My heart sank. I finished off the nuts. The lesson I learned, my friends, was do your prep work in advance, and don't let your guests wait for dinner for more than an hour and a half *tops*. And if I should come to your house for dinner, seat me far away from the nuts.

SERVES 6

## Ingredients:

**1 large orange, rind and juice**

**1 lemon, rind and half juice**

**½ cup olive oil**

**¼ cup honey**

**¼ cup brown sugar**

**3–4 good shakes white wine vinegar**

**½ pound pecans (or other nuts)**

**Packet of sweetened cranberries**

**Salt and pepper**

## Method:

Preheat oven to 350 degrees.

Mix all ingredients together, except nuts and cranberries, which you mix together in a separate bowl.

Combine the 2 bowls, spread mixture flat on cookie sheet and toast in oven for around 20 minutes.

# BASIL LEMON PESTO

In summer, when the basil abounds in our vegetable garden, there is nothing I love more than pesto. In London, sometime in the mid '90s, pesto hit. Every time you went to anyone's house for dinner, you were served pasta with pesto sauce. It was delicious, but by the five hundredth time, I never wanted to look at pesto again.

I took a very long break and came back to pesto a few years ago, realizing just how good it is thinned with olive oil and drizzled over ripe tomatoes or a summer salad. Or I add more pine nuts to keep it thick and use it as a companion for grilled fish. The recipe below is perfect for the White Fish Pesto Sandwich (page 114).

Although I usually associate pesto with summer, in winter, thickened with pine nuts, it becomes a surprisingly meaty addition to a meal.

MAKES 1 CUP

### Ingredients:

2 cups fresh basil leaves, packed

⅓ cup pine nuts or walnuts

3 medium-sized cloves garlic, minced

½ cup extra virgin olive oil

½ cup freshly grated Parmesan-Reggiano or Romano cheese

Zest of 1 lemon

Salt and freshly ground black pepper

### Method:

Combine the basil with the pine nuts, and pulse a few times in a food processor. Add the garlic, and pulse a few times more.

Slowly add the olive oil in a constant stream while the food processor is on. Stop to scrape down the sides of the bowl with a rubber spatula. Add the grated cheese and pulse again until blended. Add lemon zest, a pinch of salt and freshly ground black pepper to taste.

# VEGAN SPINACH QUICHE
# WITH HERB AND QUINOA CRUST

I might be the faddiest food person I know. No one ever knows what to cook for me, because they have no idea which particular fad I'll be following at any given moment. I have been vegan, eating no animal products whatsoever, before swinging back to the other extreme and eating only animal protein and vegetables. I have been raw, done nothing but juicing, removed refined carbohydrates, removed all carbohydrates and had no dairy . . . it is exhausting.

But good food is good food. I created this recipe during my vegan phase, and it was one of the better ones. The ESPN host Mike Greenberg, known to his fans as Greeny, still, embarrassingly, talks publicly about the disaster that was my lima bean casserole. I think he may secretly have quite enjoyed it, but his stomach? Apparently it was the casserole that kept on giving.

The filling of this quiche is so delicious, I promise you won't miss the butter, eggs and cream. You could absolutely use a whole wheat pastry crust—I just try to avoid flour when I can choose something that's better nutritionally, and quinoa is such a superfood, as are flaxseeds, I thought I'd try it. It worked perfectly.

My favorite part is adding turmeric. If it were white, I guarantee it wouldn't be as convincing, but it turns a lovely eggy pale yellow, flecked all over with the green spinach. This has to be one of my favorite recipes.

# VEGAN SPINACH QUICHE WITH HERB AND QUINOA CRUST

SERVES 4–6

## Ingredients for Crust:

1 cup cooked quinoa

2 tablespoons flaxseeds

Small bunch of basil and thyme, finely chopped

Salt and pepper

2 tablespoons quinoa/spelt/rice/whole wheat flour to bind (you may need a little more or less)

## Method for Crust:

Mix quinoa, flaxseeds and herbs together, and add seasoning to taste. Grease a flan tin with a removable base and press the quinoa mixture firmly and evenly over the base and up the sides.

## Ingredients for Filling:

1 package firm tofu, drained

1 clove garlic, minced

½ teaspoon turmeric (for color)

½ teaspoon sea salt

½ teaspoon nutmeg

¼ cup nutritional yeast

1 teaspoon Dijon mustard

Juice of ½ lemon

5–6 cups fresh spinach

¼ cup roasted pine nuts (from Trader Joes, or toast regular pine nuts on a dry skillet, turning constantly until brown)

## Method for Filling:

Preheat oven to 350 degrees.

Combine tofu through lemon in a blender and purée until smooth. Add spinach leaves and pulse until blended. Pour into base, sprinkle pine nuts over top and bake 30–40 minutes. Serve warm or cold.

# TOMATO TARTE TATIN

My father claims to be a wonderful cook. He does, in fact, have a few dishes that he makes spectacularly well and tarte Tatin is one of them.

Growing up, we had a house in France and every vacation was spent hopping on a plane to France, to our very old stone farmhouse nestled in the hills, gathering olives from the orchard and taking them down to Opio to be turned into olive oil, and watching the grown-ups sit outside under pergolas dripping with wisteria, drinking rosé and eating wonderful pâtés and cheeses.

Finishing, almost always, with my father's traditional apple tarte Tatin.

I decided to experiment with tomatoes, a little less sugar, some balsamic vinegar, and it has now become a staple. We eat it mostly in summer with tomatoes picked fresh from the garden, but it is substantial and comforting enough to work beautifully in winter, too.

SERVES 6

**Ingredients:**

½ cup (1 stick) butter

2 tablespoons brown sugar

1 tablespoon balsamic vinegar

8–12 medium tomatoes, sliced

1 sheet frozen puff pastry, thawed

Bunch of fresh basil, julienned

Method:

Preheat oven to 350 degrees.

Melt the butter in a large skillet over low heat. Add sugar and cook until it begins to thicken. Add balsamic vinegar. Layer tomatoes over mixture in circles, overlapping, starting from the outside in.

Lay pastry sheet gently over top, tucking sides in with a knife. Make sure the overhang is no more than ½".

Put pan in oven for around 30 minutes or until pastry is nicely browned.

Remove from oven and place a plate over the top, making sure it covers most of the pastry but fits inside the pan.

Holding plate tightly, flip the pan so the plate is on the bottom.

Garnish with fresh basil.

# FIG AND CAMEMBERT TARTS

I am obsessed with figs. A few years ago we fell in love with a beautiful piece of land by the beach in Westport, Connecticut. It had a somewhat dilapidated house on it and a gorgeous mature fig tree, weeping with figs that looked like they would have been ready about three weeks after closing. We signed contracts on the house, knowing we would tear down what was there and build what we thought of as a *new old house*—a house that may have been new, but would look and feel as if it had been there for years.

I was overwhelmed by the thought of building from scratch, but hugely excited about the lovely old fig tree. I got busy gathering fig recipes, including this one. I planned fig jam, fig tarts and all kinds of fig compotes. On the day we closed, I excitedly drove over to the house, frowning as I walked up the garden. Was it my imagination or had the fig tree miraculously disappeared? It turns out, the fig tree had been dug out of the ground by the previous owners just before we closed, hence our naming the house Figless Manor.

At least the recipes didn't go to waste, and we planted a new, tiny fig tree to see the land into the future. All summer long, I serve figs in salads. I'll chuck in handfuls of toasted nuts, some goat cheese and serve with simple French dressing and good bread.

But salads are never enough for me in winter. In winter, I want hot food, with crumbly, buttery pastry that melts in your mouth. I want food that's sweet and savory, that makes me feel like wherever I am, I'm home. And I want something substantial, which is why I love serving tarts to start.

This is one of those dishes that makes you feel all the above things, and makes you long for summer when the fig trees will be dripping with fruit. I know the original recipe came from a magazine, possibly *Hello!*, but I have not been able to track it down.

# FIG AND CAMEMBERT TARTS

SERVES 4–6

## Ingredients:

½ cup (1 stick) butter

1 cup all-purpose flour

1 teaspoon salt

½ cup iced water

### Filling:

1 cup heavy cream

2 sprigs thyme

1 tablespoon Dijon mustard

Salt and pepper

2 whole Camembert cheeses, broken into pieces

4 egg yolks

1 egg

4 ripe figs, halved

### Dressing:

¼ cup chopped hazelnuts

Large bunch of flat-leaf parsley, chopped

1 teaspoon Dijon mustard

Juice of ½ lemon

1 tablespoon red wine vinegar

Salt and pepper

½ cup extra virgin olive oil

## Method:

Preheat oven to 350 degrees.

Dice butter and add to a food processor with flour and salt. Pulse gently until it is like damp sand. Very slowly, pour enough iced water in to bring the dough together. Cover in plastic wrap and refrigerate for half an hour.

Grease a 9" tart pan with removable base. Roll out pastry and gently lay in tart pan, pressing into all corners, and trimming off excess. Prick base all over with a fork. Chill in fridge.

Gently heat the cream on the stove with the thyme, Dijon mustard, salt and pepper. Drop Camembert pieces into cream. Remove from heat while cheese melts.

Blind bake the pastry crust by lining it with greaseproof paper, pouring in either dry beans or rice and cooking in oven for 8–10 minutes.

Crack 4 egg yolks and 1 whole egg into a bowl and slowly pour the cream mixture over them, stirring all the time so as not to cook the eggs with the hot liquid. Season with salt and black pepper.

Turn the oven down to 320 degrees. Pour the mixture into the pastry crust and place the 8 fig halves cut-side up. Make sure this is done in a way that, when the tart is sliced, each portion has its own fig.

Place the pastry crust back into the oven and cook for 20–25 minutes, or until the mixture has set.

Prepare the dressing while the tart is cooking. Chop the hazelnuts and the parsley. Combine in a bowl with the Dijon mustard, lemon juice and red wine vinegar. Season with salt and pepper before slowly adding in the olive oil, mixing all the time until smooth.

Once cooked, leave to cool for about half an hour before slicing and serving with the vinaigrette drizzled over top.

# ROASTED CAULIFLOWER WITH OLIVE AND LEMON VINAIGRETTE

Last year, I discovered the reason that I was so exhausted all the time and had put on a substantial amount of weight that wouldn't shift was the double whammy of not only Lyme disease, but Hashimoto's disease, which means I don't produce enough thyroid hormones.

I tell you this only because for months, I had been furiously juicing vast amounts of kale in a bid to get better, plus eating the only vegetables I really enjoy—broccoli and cauliflower. It turns out that large quantities of cruciferous vegetables, namely kale, broccoli and cauliflower, are pretty much disastrous for your thyroid, and helped suppress what little thyroid activity I had left.

I stopped with the vegetables, but when I do eat them, this is what I eat. It's perfect as a starter for a dinner party, being both pretty and surprising.

SERVES 4

## Ingredients:

1 medium head cauliflower

2 tablespoons olive oil

Salt and pepper

## Vinaigrette:

1 clove garlic, minced

Salt

2 tablespoons white wine vinegar

2 tablespoons extra virgin olive oil

¼ cup finely chopped black olives pitted (the wrinkly ones, not kalamata)

Zest of 1 lemon

Juice of ½ lemon

1 tablespoon chopped flat-leaf parsley

⅛ teaspoon red chili flakes

## Method:

Preheat oven to 450 degrees.

Remove leaves from cauliflower then cut into slices, top to bottom, around ¼" thick, so they are almost like a steak.

Arrange in layer on baking sheet, brush with olive oil, season. Roast 15–20 minutes, then turn over and roast other side.

To make vinaigrette, mash garlic and salt with vinegar, whisk in olive oil until thick, add olives, lemon zest, juice, parsley and red chili flakes.

Serve cauliflower hot with drizzled dressing.

# FRENCH ONION SOUP

I recently flipped through the Junior League cookbook for inspiration and settled upon French Onion Soup for dinner, because it's freezing and there's nothing quite like French Onion Soup, oozing with gruyére cheese, to warm you up.

I added some thyme and red wine. Many recipes call for the addition of cognac, brandy, sherry or white wine, but you work with what you have. It is also fine to leave out the alcohol altogether. I wish I had put the thyme in a small bag of cheesecloth (or one of those gauze bandages we all have in the back of the first aid cupboard), tied up with string. I ended up fishing it out rather carefully, as I realized it felt a bit like crunching down on potpourri.

One last thing. In flipping through the Junior League cookbook, I noticed there is a recipe for Narcissa Titman's Curried Pea Soup. I love Curried Pea Soup (see page 40). It's one of my favorite recipes in the world, mostly because of how easy it is to make, and because I love the name Narcissa Titman. I am very tempted to write a character called Narcissa Titman, except I think she might sue. I digress. As much as I love Curried Pea Soup, nothing, absolutely nothing, beats French Onion Soup.

Let's be honest here. Is there anything more comforting on a cold winter's night, when you're tired or depressed or a bit low, than a big bowl of French Onion Soup, the cheese dripping in gooey strands from the toasted baguette floating on top? In all honesty, my first port of call on those cold winter's nights for a touch of comfort does tend to be a cup of tea, because a proper cup of tea—English breakfast, sweet, milky—is, for we English, the ultimate panacea for anything and everything that ails us.

But French Onion Soup is a pretty close second, not least because it's fantastically easy to make and is more than enough for an entire meal. I have served this many times with just a large green salad, and all of us are entirely sated by the end of the meal.

# FRENCH ONION SOUP

SERVES 4

### Ingredients:

½ cup (1 stick) butter

4 onions, thinly sliced

1 tablespoon brown sugar

4 cups beef stock

1 cup red wine (or brandy, cognac, sherry or white wine)

Salt and pepper

Thyme

Dash of Worcestershire sauce

1 baguette

Grated gruyère cheese

Olive oil

Grated parmesan cheese

### Method:

Melt the butter in a large heavy pan (I use a Le Creuset, which is perfect) and add the onions, stirring constantly on low heat until they are soft and caramelizing—around 20 minutes.

Add brown sugar. Stir. Add stock, wine and seasoning. Bring to boil, cover and simmer for half an hour to an hour. Add Worcestershire sauce.

When ready to serve, slice and toast baguette. Ladle soup into bowls and cover each with thick handful of gruyère. Top with slice of toast, drizzle with olive oil, sprinkle with parmesan then run under broiler to melt and brown.

# SWEET CORN AND CHILI SOUP

The first time I grew corn, the Smalls were truly tiny. Growing up in London, I dreamed of growing corn, and I will never forget the first time I picked a cob fresh from my garden. I sank my teeth in, amazed at the sweetness of freshly picked corn, that instant rush of sugar before it all turns to starch.

This is one of my mum's brilliant recipes. In actual fact, you don't even need the onion, garlic and celery. If you were to cook the corn in stock, add the chili, seasoning and half-and-half, I promise you it would be just as good.

Just so you know, I have lied frequently at dinner parties when asked for the recipe, and pretended I have cooked fresh ears of corn then meticulously cut all the kernels off. I have not. Ever. I have only ever made this with frozen corn, and I feel much better now that I have confessed.

It can be jazzed up by garnishing with a few kernels of corn roasted in olive oil until golden brown.

SERVES 4–6

## Ingredients:

1 medium white onion, chopped

2 tablespoons butter

2 cloves garlic, chopped

2 stalks celery, chopped

½ medium red chili or dried chili flakes to taste

1 bag frozen corn kernels

1 quart vegetable stock

Salt and pepper

½ cup half-and-half

## Method:

In a large pan, soften the onions in butter, add garlic after 1 minute and celery 1 minute later. Cook gently for around 5 minutes until soft. Add chili, frozen corn and vegetable stock. Season well with salt and pepper.

Bring to boil, then cover and turn down to simmer for half an hour.

Take off heat, purée soup with handheld blender. Add half-and-half at end and garnish with slices of red chili or kernels of roasted corn.

# CAULIFLOWER AND PARMIGIANO SOUP WITH TRUFFLE OIL

This soup was a happy mistake. It came from one of those nights where I didn't seem to have anything in the fridge other than a head of cauliflower that was well on its way to becoming inedible, a packet of pancetta and some stale parmesan.

I do always tend to have onions, garlic, carrots and cauliflower, and always stock in the pantry. When all else fails, I can always pull something together with the aforementioned and anything else I can find.

This was that night, and the truffle oil added the most delicious twist. For a whole winter, we ended up eating this almost every night.

SERVES 4–6

## Ingredients:

2 ounces chopped pancetta

1 cup chopped onion

3 cloves garlic, chopped

¾ cup chopped celery

1 head cauliflower

3½ cups chicken broth

1" cube parmigiano,
or any other strong cheese
(reserve some cheese to
sprinkle over the top to serve)

½ cup half-and-half

White or black truffle oil
for drizzling

## Method:

Sauté pancetta until brown. Add onion, garlic and celery and cook until vegetables are soft—a little over 5 minutes. Add cauliflower, broth and cheese. Bring to boil and simmer, covered, for around 20 minutes.

Purée soup with a handheld blender, then add half-and-half. When ready to serve, ladle into bowls, drizzle with truffle oil and sprinkle cheese on top.

I made this with gorgonzola recently and it was *amazing*.

# CURRIED PEA SOUP

Another one of my mum's standbys, and yet another that you can make with just the peas cooked in stock, curry powder and something creamy to finish.

Narcissa Titman makes it with a French base called a *mire-poix*, which is the standard base of all French stock and the foundation of most soups: finely diced onions, carrots and celery. But I wasn't interested in the recipe (although I'm sure it's delicious). I was interested in her name, as mentioned previously.

(Whoops. Just back from googling Ms. Titman. She is friends with Amanda Hesser who is a fabulous food writer. I have all Amanda Hesser's books and recommend them hugely—and seems Ms. Titman is a wonderful cook. May now have to—gasp—roll up my sleeves and get working, finely chopping those vegetables for the mire-poix to try out her recipe).

Although this recipe is perfectly good as is.

SERVES 4

## Ingredients:

1 onion, finely chopped

2 tablespoons butter

Olive oil

1 bag frozen peas

3–4 cups chicken or vegetable stock

Salt and pepper

1 teaspoon each of curry powder, cumin and ground coriander

Crème fraiche or sour cream

## Method:

Soften a finely chopped onion in butter and a dash of oil. Add peas and stock.

Simmer until peas are tender, then purée with a handheld blender. Season with salt and pepper to taste and add spices. Simmer on very low heat to let spices absorb.

Serve with dollop of crème fraiche or sour cream.

# CURRIED PARSNIP AND APPLE SOUP

Every Thanksgiving, I vow that next year I will find a willing friend to host us and our enormous tribe, and every year, I end up gathering family and friends, with assorted waifs and strays, and doing it myself.

For a few years, I collapsed at the table, exhausted, barely able to keep my eyes open, until I realized I had to print out a timeline. Now, I start the preparation three days before, so by the time Thanksgiving arrives, everything is done, and I can actually enjoy myself.

The beauty of this soup, which has become our mainstay, is that it gets better with time. Make it the day before and the spices really come out. Omit the cream and it doesn't really get healthier.

SERVES 6

## Ingredients:

1 tablespoon butter

1 pound parsnips, peeled and cut into chunks

2 apples, peeled, cored and sliced

2 stalks celery, finely chopped

1 medium onion, chopped

2 teaspoons curry powder

1 teaspoon ground cumin

1 teaspoon ground coriander

1 clove garlic, crushed

4 cups good chicken or vegetable stock

Salt and pepper

¼ cup heavy cream

Small bunch of chives, finely chopped

Thinly sliced apples, sautéed in butter until golden to garnish (optional)

## Method:

Heat the butter and, when foaming, add parsnips, apples, celery and onions, and soften them without letting them change color.

Add curry, cumin, coriander and garlic and cook for about 2 minutes, stirring all the time. Add the stock, bring to boil, cover and turn down to simmer gently for half an hour or until parsnips are soft. Purée with handheld blender and add more stock if too thick. Season with salt and pepper to taste. Add cream. Garnish with chopped·chives, and apples, if using.

# ZUCCHINI SOUP

I really dislike zucchini. I dislike it steamed, sautéed, fried. It's always too watery for my taste, and yet when it transforms into either zucchini bread or zucchini soup, I love it.

Last summer, friends brought over a giant zucchini from their garden. It was the biggest thing I had ever seen. I took it with me when I went to an old barn in Vermont that I had rented for a week in order to get some quiet, distraction-free writing done.

That zucchini served me for lunch and dinner for the entire week. I can't exactly say I loved it, but slathered in olive oil and salt, sautéed to a golden brown, it was a very welcome gift.

This, however, takes the humble zucchini to a whole other level. It is one of those surprising recipes that reads as rather dull and probably not something you would make, and yet it is absurdly good, transforming into the most delicious soup.

SERVES 4

**Ingredients:**

1½ pounds chopped zucchini

2 tablespoons olive oil

2 cloves garlic, minced

3 cups chicken stock

Salt and pepper

1 tablespoon chopped flat-leaf parsley

1 cup grated parmesan cheese

**Method:**

Soften the zucchini in olive oil over low heat for about 20 minutes, adding the garlic halfway through.

Add the stock, season with salt and pepper, bring to a boil, then immediately turn down to a simmer for around 5 minutes.

Remove from heat and purée with a handheld blender until smooth.

Add parsley and parmesan.

Serve with hot, crusty bread.

# COUNTRY BEAN AND PESTO SOUP

Anything that uses up those cans that multiply in my pantry can only be a good thing. And Italian country-style food is always a win.

Years ago, when I was a budding author, I was sent to the Penguin sales conference in Spain. There was a new, hot, young chef there who none of us had ever heard of, but who had a cookbook coming out. We all fell instantly in love with him.

His name was Jamie Oliver, and he was on the cusp of soaring to fame with a TV show and his simple country Italian food. We went out to lunch by a harbor somewhere and I ordered asparagus. When it arrived, I took a bite without even looking at it. Jamie leaned over and asked, "How is it?"

"Delicious," I replied, as a reflex.

"Really?" He frowned. "Isn't it tinned?" I looked down at my plate of fleshy, congealed, pale, tasteless asparagus, and instantly turned beet red. It was pretty disgusting. I mumbled something about a good sauce. I still blush when I think about it.

Happily, should Jamie Oliver ever find himself in your part of the world and hungry for dinner, this is something you could serve him in a heartbeat.

SERVES 6

### Ingredients:

2 tablespoons olive oil

1 onion, chopped

4 cloves garlic, crushed

2 carrots, chopped

2 stalks celery, chopped

2 shakes Sriracha or Tabasco

2 cans cannellini beans

4 cups chicken or vegetable stock

1 small can tomatoes

1 bay leaf (optional)

4 tablespoons pesto

½ teaspoon thyme

4 tablespoons grated parmesan

Salt and pepper

½ cup roasted peppers (optional)

### Method:

Heat olive oil in pan and add onions, softening. Add garlic after about 5 minutes and continue gently sautéing, adding carrots and celery. Cook for another 6–7 minutes.

Add hot sauce, cannellini beans, 1 cup stock, tomatoes, and bay leaf, if using. Bring to a boil, then immediately turn down to simmer until thickened, around 8 minutes.

Stir in 3 more cups of stock. Continue cooking another 15 minutes. Stir in pesto, thyme and cheese. Allow to melt. Season to taste.

Garnish with sprinkled thyme and a drizzle of good olive oil. If you have roasted peppers, cutting them into fine strips and stirring them in looks gorgeous.

# CAULIFLOWER AND STILTON SOUP

First, you know it's one of my made-up recipes when there are no proper measurements. Either that, or it's a recipe from my mum. I love soup, particularly thick and creamy vegetable soups that don't actually have any cream or butter, but thicken by virtue of the amount of vegetables versus stock. Soup makes me think of fall, burning log fires, kicking through leaves, cozy sweaters and scarves—my favorite time of the year.

I have used stock cubes here, which are a staple in my pantry. Knorr makes them, as does Oxo, but the very best I've ever found, the ones I look for and try to stock up on because you can't always find them, are made by a brand called Telma, which is a kosher stock cube, hence found in the kosher section of your supermarket (at least, it is in our local Stop & Shop).

SERVES 4

**Ingredients:**

2 leeks

Olive oil

1 head cauliflower, broken into florets

2 chicken stock cubes

Salt and pepper

½ cup Stilton

Crumbled Stilton, chopped chives, or 1 teaspoon crème fraiche (optional)

Method:

Slice leeks and soften in oil on gentle heat, around 10 minutes At the same time sautee the cauliflower gently in a separate pan until slightly brown (think toasted). Then add cauliflower to leeks and stir over gentle heat while leeks continue to soften.

Add 6–8 cups water.

Crumble in stock cubes and add seasoning. Bring to a boil and turn down to simmer for 20–30 minutes, until cauliflower is soft.

Blend with a handheld blender until smooth.

Add Stilton and stir.

Garnish either with crumbled Stilton, chopped chives, 1 teaspoon crème fraiche or some combination of all three.

# Middles . . .

The food I love the most for comfort are one-pot dishes. The ease of putting a ton of ingredients in a heavy French casserole and having them emerge, slow-cooked, hours later, filled with aromatics and meltingly soft meat, just makes me feel good.

These are not all one-pot dishes, but they all evoke comfort. I do tend to veer toward the spicier foods. Perhaps I'm more sensitive than most, but bland has never worked for me. I seem to be a woman of extremes—hot or cold, black or white—either direction is fine, as long as it's strong. With food, I like everything to be *tasty*—I need it to be in order to feel it or taste it.

I gravitate toward food that is spiced. Indian and Middle Eastern are often where I find comfort and hopefully you will, too.

# MOROCCAN CHICKEN

A little while ago, we had friends over for dinner, and I turned to Diana Henry for inspiration. She is an English food writer, and her books are my absolute favorite. If ever I don't know what to make, her books are the ones I turn to. In *Crazy Water, Pickled Lemons*, she uses a fair amount of Moroccan and Middle Eastern food, mixing the sweet and sour, all delicately spiced, which is the sort of food I adore. And more, I love that it's all food that can be prepared in advance—comforting tagines and casseroles, no last-minute fiddling.

I made Moroccan Chicken with tomatoes and saffron-honey jam, then berries for dessert, with figs stuffed with marzipan and almonds, dipped in chocolate, also courtesy of Diana Henry. It was all delicious.

SERVES 4–6

## Ingredients:

3 cloves garlic, minced

1½ teaspoons ground cumin

1 teaspoon ground ginger

1 teaspoon kosher salt

½ teaspoon ground turmeric

½ teaspoon paprika

¼ teaspoon ground cinnamon

Salt and pepper

4 chicken legs, rinsed and patted dry, drumsticks and thighs separated

2 tablespoons olive oil

2 onions, sliced

1 preserved lemon

1 cup Greek olives, pitted

10 dried dates, pitted and halved lengthwise

Small bunch of cilantro, finely chopped

## Method:

Combine spices and seasoning, coat chicken and place in fridge for 1 hour minimum.

When ready to cook, bring olive oil to sizzling and brown chicken in small batches, removing from pan when brown.

Add onions, and more oil if necessary, and scraping all the brown bits from the pan, cook onions gently until golden brown.

Put chicken back in pan, cover and cook on medium heat for 20 minutes.

Remove rind from lemon, discard rest and cut rind into strips.

Add lemon rind, olives and dates to chicken, stir, cover and cook another 20 minutes.

Garnish with chopped cilantro and serve with couscous or flatbread.

# PANTRY CHICKEN AND BEANS

Apparently you are not supposed to have canned beans in the pantry. This is a pity because the vast majority of shelving in my rather large pantry appears to be taken up with canned beans. With a few canned tomatoes, too. On a mission to start using up what I have, I decided to use some of the beans the other day.

There is a staggering amount of stuff in my pantry, as I may have already mentioned. My friend, who is known as the Chestnut due to her permanent, very dark suntan (and how does she manage it even in the depths of winter, I would like to know?), said it resembled Stop & Shop. Almost anything you could possibly want is in there. After reading a piece about clutter being bad for your general feng shui, I have decided not to replenish until I have used absolutely everything.

I improvised an Italian chicken and bean dish, which was delicious, and now know that nothing is essential. Use what you have, and play around. No olives? No worries. I happened to have all the ingredients at hand, but even just beans, tomatoes and chili would be delicious.

SERVES 6

### Ingredients:

Olive oil

3 cans beans (I used chick peas and black beans, and have in the past used kidney beans and lima beans)

1 can diced tomatoes

Dried chili to taste—hefty pinch is usually good

5 sun-dried tomatoes, snipped up

Handful of black olives, pitted and cut in half

4–5 anchovies, snipped up

3 cloves garlic

6 chicken breasts

Bunch of small tomatoes on the vine, if you have them (completely inessential, but pretty if you do)

### Method:

Preheat oven to 350 degrees.

Drain and rinse the beans. Oil a casserole dish, and pour beans in.

Add rest of ingredients, bar chicken and tomatoes on the vine, and fold in, being careful not to break the beans.

Add whole tomatoes.

Roast in oven for around 25 minutes, until tomatoes soften and start to smell delicious.

Heat olive oil in pan until sizzling, add chicken breasts and brown. Add chicken breasts to tomatoes, placing on top. Bake in oven for around 30 minutes more, until chicken is done.

Garnish with chopped parsley if you have any.

# ASIAN ORANGE CHICKEN

Just as every single girl I knew in London in the '90s brought out pasta and pesto sauce for every girls' dinner, every proper dinner party I went to in London during that same era made a Delia Smith dish called Chicken Basque.

For those who don't know, Delia Smith is the patron saint of cookbooks in England. She is our Julia Child, only less eccentric, and absolutely foolproof. For years, I used to invite assorted waifs and strays to my small flat in Maida Vale for Christmas, and every single thing I cooked was from Delia's Christmas cookbook. It was always and consistently delicious.

She is still my go-to for all food-related questions and her Chicken Basque, with its smoky Spanish flavor, is one of those one-pot dishes that, since I have moved to America, never fails to delight. Even more so because no one here is familiar with her food.

A few years ago, I spent months cooking for my Unwell Friend. First, for her, a multitude of vegan dishes to try to help her on the road back to health, and later, for her family. They laughed that they were the lucky recipients of my cooking therapy. It was true that I cooked for them in order to make myself feel better, but it was also my way of giving, of showing my love.

And it was because I did not know what else to do.

I had a couple of huge hits with some of the recipes. For this one, I experimented by combining an Asian orange chicken recipe with Delia's Chicken Basque, resulting in a wondrous one-pot Asian orange chicken with onions, peppers and rice.

# ASIAN ORANGE CHICKEN

SERVES 6–8

Ingredients:

Method:

2 chickens, jointed into
8 pieces, seasoned

Zest of 4 oranges

⅔ cup fresh orange juice

¼ cup honey

3 tablespoons soy sauce

2 tablespoons toasted
sesame oil

1 tablespoon minced
fresh ginger

2 teaspoons finely
minced garlic

¼ teaspoon crushed
red pepper flakes

Salt and pepper

2 large red bell peppers

2 medium onions

3 tablespoons olive oil

2 cloves garlic

1 cup short-grain brown rice

1½ cups chicken stock

¾ cup dry white wine

1 teaspoon tomato paste

½ large orange, cut into ½"
wedges, peel on

4 scallions (white bulbs and
3" green), thinly sliced on
diagonal for garnish

Rinse and dry chicken pieces and combine orange zest and juice, honey, soy sauce, sesame oil, ginger, garlic and red pepper flakes into a bowl for marinade. Stir well, coat chicken pieces and refrigerate at least 1 hour, or preferably overnight.

When ready to cook, season the chicken pieces with salt and pepper. Next, slice the red peppers in half and remove the seeds and pith, then slice each half into 6 strips. Likewise, peel the onion and slice into strips of approximately the same size.

Heat 2 tablespoons of olive oil in the casserole and, when it is fairly hot, add the chicken pieces—2 or 3 at a time—and brown them to a nutty golden color on both sides. As they brown, move them to a plate lined with paper towels, using a slotted spoon. Next add remaining oil to the casserole, with the heat slightly higher than medium. As soon as the oil is hot, add the onion and peppers and allow them to brown a little at the edges, moving them around from time to time, for about 5 minutes.

After that add the garlic and toss around for a minute or 2 until the garlic is pale golden, then stir in the rice and, when the grains have a good coating of oil, add the stock, wine and tomato paste. As soon as everything has reached a simmer, turn the heat down to a gentle simmer. Add a little more seasoning, then place the chicken gently on top of everything (it's important to keep the rice down in the liquid). Finally, scatter the wedges of orange in among them.

Cover with a tight-fitting lid and cook over the gentlest possible heat for 50 minutes to 1 hour, or until the rice is cooked, but still retains a little bite. Alternatively, cook in a preheated oven at 350 degrees for 1 hour.

Garnish with scallions.

# CURRIED CREAMY CHICKEN

The absolute best part of a book tour is going to places you might not usually get to and seeing family and old friends. This past tour, I spent five full days in Los Angeles catching up with friends I have known almost my entire life. Nothing was more energizing than making those lovely, long-ago connections again.

A few summers ago, I remember driving down to BookHampton in Sag Harbor, New York, for an event—small but sweet—and the best thing of all was staying in Amagansett with a cousin of my husband.

I have to admit to a few nerves when we got there. Cousin had left the door open and told us we were staying in the "family room." We walked through the kitchen, saying hello to the two large poodles, and walked into the only room that could possibly have been a family room. It was crammed with furniture, sofas, chairs, boxes, books.

"Where are we supposed to sleep?" I whispered, my face falling along with my dreams of fluffy down pillows and soft mattresses.

"Um, floor, maybe?" Beloved said, uncertainly, as my heart plummeted.

I am a hotel snob. In fact, I rarely stay with people because I would much rather (a) be on my own and (b) stay in a luxurious hotel room, complete with room service (hopefully). I'd given up a luxury hotel room for a hard floor and I wasn't happy. But, family is family, and I figured it was only one night, and I'd survive.

We went to do the event, then out for dinner with more friends, before heading back to the house where I discovered, with enormous relief, I had gotten it entirely wrong.

The family room was a large and gorgeous bedroom downstairs, filled with photographs and letters and memorabilia of four generations of my husband's family. Both of us slept better than we had in years.

On Sunday, we had a brief wander round Amagansett, and I remembered exactly why I had fallen in love with it all those years ago—as a teen I summered there, and I am sure that's when I decided that one day I would live in America.

We hit horrible traffic on Sunday, and got back to Connecticut about 10 minutes before a gang of friends arrived for dinner. It was meant to be a barbeque, but I realized we were out of gas so I had to improvise. I made one of my mum's dishes that I haven't made in about 15 years, but it was still completely delicious—so delicious in fact, that I'm giving it to you now.

# CURRIED CREAMY CHICKEN

SERVES 6

### Ingredients:

3–4 packages frozen chopped spinach, thawed and squeezed dry

Salt and pepper

Butter

4 boneless chicken breasts

1 cup plain Greek yogurt

1 cup mayonnaise

2 tablespoons heavy cream

1 teaspoon curry powder

½ teaspoon cumin

½ teaspoon coriander

Panko bread crumbs

### Method:

Spread spinach thickly over a square ovenproof dish. Season and dot with butter.

Cut 4 chicken breasts into large chunks and poach gently in boiling water until just cooked.

Mix together Greek yogurt, mayonnaise and heavy cream to thin. Season liberally with curry powder, a little cumin and ground coriander.

Cover spinach with chicken and season. Pour mayonnaise mix over the top.

Cover with bread crumbs, and cook at 350 degrees for 30–40 minutes, until slightly browned.

# GINGER AND HONEY CHICKEN WITH SOY

This is one of those dishes that involves things I can always find in my kitchen. I keep chicken breasts in the freezer at all times, just in case, along with cubes of chopped ginger and garlic.

I have not served this at a dinner party, and honestly, I'm not sure I would, unless it were a casual kitchen supper. This has become our staple for last-minute suppers for the kids, and I say "last minute" because I almost never have the time or patience to marinate for an hour, what with starving children everywhere. Even marinating for 5 minutes produces an impressively delicious result for a family supper.

# GINGER AND HONEY CHICKEN WITH SOY

SERVES 4

## Ingredients:

2 tablespoons runny honey

2 tablespoons soy sauce

1 tablespoon Dijon mustard

2 tablespoons olive oil

3 cloves garlic, chopped

1 tablespoon grated fresh ginger, or 1 teaspoon ground ginger

4 boneless, skinless chicken breasts

Salt and pepper

1 large onion, sliced

## Method:

Mix honey, soy sauce, mustard, 1 tablespoon oil, garlic and ginger together and pour over chicken. Turn chicken over until well coated, season with salt and pepper and place in fridge at least 1 hour.

Heat 1 tablespoon oil in a skillet and, when very hot, add the chicken breasts. Leave to brown for a couple of minutes, then turn over to brown other side. Remove chicken and set aside. Add onions and more oil if necessary and fry them gently until they start to brown. Turn heat down, add chicken back to pan with sauce and allow to simmer for around 30 minutes. Add 2–3 tablespoons of water if there is not enough liquid.

Serve with white rice.

# EASY SPICED CURRY

I made this for the first time when my children were small enough for me to call them the Smalls, and their palates unsophisticated enough for me to worry that enticing them to eat anything other than pizza or chicken nuggets was a challenge I was never sure I was quite ready for.

I did manage to put one of the twins, who I used to refer to as the Maniac, off eating chicken nuggets for life by telling him they use the whole chicken: beak, feet, eyeballs, etc. I think that's true.

I once saw a TV show where Jamie Oliver was showing kids what goes into chicken nuggets, and he stuffed an entire chicken, beak, eyes, feet, bones, everything, into a blender, and pressed Start. You can imagine the shouts of disgust. When those kids were next presented with a choice of chicken nuggets or grilled chicken breast, every single one chose the chicken breast.

I wonder whether it's the association as well. Most kids don't tend to think of chickens as, well, *chickens*, until they see a whole one stuffed into a blender.

Mine of course would be the exception. A few years ago, after the ex-husband went hunting one day, the Brainiac (aka Twin B) asked me when he could go out and shoot a chicken to eat for dinner. I didn't bother responding *never*. I always wanted chickens, but to collect the eggs, not to chase them round the garden with a rifle.

Actually, when I had the farm, I did want to do the whole self-sufficiency thing, but I'm sure I couldn't actually have ever gone through with killing anything. I once went fishing with my family in the Bahamas, this was a couple of years ago, and we used tiny fish as bait and had to thread the hook through the fish's eyes to keep them on.

It was *disgusting*.

*And* they were already dead.

My parents spent the entire time roaring with laughter at my face and taking lots of pictures of me grimacing with horror as I attempted to do this without throwing up.

I didn't catch anything.

I kill nothing. Except mosquitos and flies. Everything else I catch and let free, including spiders. One Halloween, the dog woke me up at midnight by barking at something in the corner of the bedroom. When I went to investigate, I found a bat scuttling in the corner. I swear this is true. On Halloween there truly was a bat in our bedroom. I was too tired to deal with it, so I stuck a bucket over it and went back to sleep. In the morning, I thought it was dead, so very gingerly I put it in a plastic bag. A friend came over, who happens to be the daughter of a vet.

"It's alive!" she said, in horror, noticing, I presume, the bag steaming up from the bat's breathing. "Get it out of the bag!"

So we tipped the bat into a cardboard box where it yawned and stretched, showing us its quite impressive wingspan, then it hung upside down in the box and went to sleep. It was actually extraordinary, and I felt privileged to see a bat that close up. The next morning it had gone.

Good job the Brainiac didn't see it or we would doubtless have been sitting down to Bat Bolognese.

# EASY SPICED CURRY

SERVES 4

## Ingredients:

2 tablespoons butter

Olive oil

2 medium onions, peeled and sliced

1 clove garlic, minced

2" piece ginger, peeled and grated

1 teaspoon ground cumin

15 cardamom pods, seeds removed and crushed

½ teaspoon ground turmeric

½ teaspoon chili powder

½ teaspoon cinnamon

2 bay leaves

1 bag baby spinach

¼ cup pine nuts (optional, and I would use toasted)

Handful of golden sultanas (optional)

1 cup plain Greek yogurt

1 cup crème fraiche

2 cooked chicken breasts, diced

Salt and pepper

2 tablespoons chopped cilantro (optional)

## Method:

Melt butter, add dash of oil to stop butter from burning, add onions, garlic and ginger and cook until golden.

Add spices and bay leaves (I didn't have any though), continue frying, stirring regularly, for 2–3 minutes.

Add spinach and stir so it wilts and cooks, add pine nuts and sultanas if using. Mix yogurt and crème fraiche together and stir in, add chicken, salt and pepper.

# GINGER ALMOND CHICKEN

As usual, we had a pack of people in recently for a casual supper, and I turned to one of the Barefoot Contessa books for inspiration. For a long time I didn't really "get" the Barefoot Contessa. I was wary of cooking her recipes because I was convinced everyone would be too familiar with her food.

I went to a barbecue recently and there was a dish—admittedly, delicious—of coleslaw, and all the girls asked, "Is it Ina's?" as if Ina was a friend, and not, in fact, the Barefoot Contessa herself. I found it really strange, until I remembered that once upon a time I was a Delia Smith devotee, and everything I cooked was "Delia's."

I still do, a lot of the time. She's English, and I like the fact that people don't walk in and say, "Oh, delicious, is it Delia's?" as they would in the UK. In fact, for a few years, you couldn't walk ten steps without tripping over her Chicken Basque. (It's still the most delicious dish of all time, but it did get a bit tiresome after a while, eating it over and over and over again.)

Then came Jamie Oliver, then Nigella and now, thankfully, there are enough wonderful cookbooks that you don't get served the same dish for dinner every time you go to someone's house.

So as I was looking for inspiration recently, I read some of Ina Garten's philosophy. What she writes in her book on parties is that so much of cooking is about organization. She tells of times when she has slaved over the stove, not being able to enjoy her guests. Now the only way she cooks is to have everything done in advance so she can effectively be a guest at her own party. I couldn't agree more, and I am a new convert.

This is one of those dishes that can be easily done in advance. This is not my recipe, and I have no idea where it comes from, but thank you to whoever was clever enough to come up with it.

# GINGER ALMOND CHICKEN

SERVES 6–8

## Ingredients:

2 teaspoons ground coriander

1 teaspoon grated fresh ginger

2 teaspoons white wine vinegar

½ teaspoon salt

¼ teaspoon pepper

4 teaspoons vegetable oil

4 chicken breasts, boneless and skinless, cut into cubes

½ cup mango chutney

¼ cup chicken stock

1 teaspoon crushed garlic

4 scallions, chopped

¼ cup fresh ginger peeled and julienned

¼ cup sliced almonds, toasted

Small bunch of cilantro, chopped

## Method:

Stir together the coriander, grated ginger, vinegar, salt, pepper and 2 teaspoons of oil. Add the chicken cubes and stir well to combine. Marinate for around 1 hour in the fridge.

In a bowl, combine the mango chutney, chicken stock and garlic.

Heat the remaining oil in a wok or skillet, add the scallions and julienned ginger, fry on high heat for 30 seconds. Add the chicken and stir-fry until cooked, around 6 more minutes. Add the chutney and stock mix and continue cooking for 2 more minutes.

Garnish with the toasted almond and chopped cilantro and serve with white rice.

# PORK AND LEMON PATTIES

I am firmly of the belief that adding lemon zest to pretty much everything elevates it to a whole other level. These are like little sophisticated meatballs, perfect in a bigger size for dinner, but even better, I think, when small and served as an hors d'oeuvre.

Nigel Slater makes these with parmesan and anchovies, but I prefer gruyère, and although I adore anchovies, not everyone does, and they don't seem to disappear in this recipe in the way they so often do with lamb. An unlucky bite can result in a mouthful of anchovy, and even if you are passionate about them, as I am, it isn't a pleasant experience.

SERVES 6

### Ingredients:

Zest of 1 lemon

1 pound minced pork

½ cup panko bread crumbs

Juice of 1 lemon

Large bunch of flat-leaf parsley

2 cups fresh basil leaves

2 heaping tablespoons grated gruyère

Salt and pepper

4 tablespoons olive oil

1 cup chicken stock

### Dipping Sauce:

½ cup plain Greek yogurt

½ cup mayonnaise

2 cloves garlic, minced

Handful of parsley, grated

Salt and pepper

### Method:

Grate zest of lemon into pork and bread crumbs. Add lemon juice, roughly chopped parsley and basil, and gruyère. Season generously and mix.

Make about 25 balls, roughly a heaped tablespoon, and flatten slightly.

Roll in bread crumbs, heat oil, and fry in small batches for 4–5 minutes on each side. Do *not* crowd the pan. When all are browned, pour in stock, bring to boil, and simmer for 20 minutes.

For sauce, combine all ingredients and mix well.

# TOAD IN THE HOLE

When the Eldest Son finished Roald Dahl's *Danny the Champion of the World*, his overwhelming memory of it was all the mouthwatering descriptions of the food. Thus far he has had me promise to make him Toad in the Hole and an authentic Game Pie, complete with boiled eggs hidden in the meat, just as Roald Dahl describes.

Toad in the Hole, for those who don't know, is essentially a pan of Yorkshire pudding—the American equivalent is the popover—with sizzling pork sausages dotted around. It's one of those comfort foods we associate with childhood, together with dishes like Shepherd's pie, rice pudding and custard, and steak and kidney pudding.

My *most* favorite thing in the world when I was at school was the skin off the top of the custard. This was a rare treat. Every day the lunch lady would ask for a show of hands, and dozens of jiggling children would try to catch her attention so they could be the one to have the delicious custard skin.

I remember things like treacle tart and cornflake tart. A peculiar chocolate pudding with a not-very-nice chocolate custard. Of course, there was spotted dick and custard—a sponge pudding dotted with raisins, which all Americans find singularly hilarious.

Here is my favorite Toad in the Hole recipe.

SERVES 4–6

### Ingredients:

1½ cups all-purpose flour

1 teaspoon kosher salt

Black pepper for seasoning

3 eggs, beaten

1½ cups milk

2 tablespoons melted butter

1 tablespoon vegetable oil (not extra-virgin olive oil)

8 sausages, preferably pork

### Method:

Preheat oven to 425 degrees.

In a bowl whisk flour, salt and pepper.

Make a well in center of flour, pour in eggs, milk and melted butter. Whisk in with flour until smooth. Cover and let stand for 1 hour.

Add oil to skillet. Add sausages and brown on all sides.

Coat bottom and sides of a heavy dish with oil. (Never use extra-virgin, which has an extremely low flash point, and should not be used in frying-hot cooking.)

Put dish in hot oven and wait for the oil to heat (or use a heavy Le Creuset pan and heat the oil on the stove top). As soon as the oil sizzles, add the sausages, then pour the batter over.

Cook for 25–30 minutes, or until the batter is golden and puffy.

# MAPLE PORK CHOPS

I think this is from *Food and Wine* magazine. I am not entirely sure because I found it stuck into my recipe book. I have made it many times. Have I mentioned that I love pork? I tried going vegan, I tried going raw, I tried going vegetarian, but each time, it was the pork that undid me.

I wish I was someone who loved fish. Or salads. (Although I do quite like salads.) But ultimately, I am a tremendous carnivore. If you believe in Peter d'Adamo's theory of eating right for your blood type, as O Rhesus Negative, I am, apparently, an inherent meat eater.

My son is sixteen years old and at the age where he really should think everything his mother does is painfully embarrassing. The truth is, he does think that most of what I do is painfully embarrassing (this includes singing very loudly in the car, quizzing new friends all about their lives, and particularly, complaining in a restaurant). But the one thing he always gives me massive props for is the ability to open a fridge that appears to be almost empty and create a delicious meal out of nothing.

I will say, it is one of my superpowers, and I'm not sure where it comes from. Because my parents were war babies, I think the need to use up every last drop was instilled very early, and I don't feel calm unless I know that absolutely nothing has gone to waste.

All these ingredients, bar the pork chops, are things I keep in the pantry as a matter of course. I have pots of rosemary outside, and thyme lining the path, which can serve as the bare minimum to jazz up anything. This is a lovely way of sprucing up boring old pork chops, and the maple syrup glaze is sublime.

SERVES 4–6

## Ingredients:

½ cup pecans

½ cup pure maple syrup

⅛ cup cider vinegar

1 tablespoon Dijon mustard

½ teaspoon Sriracha

3" sprig rosemary

6 pork loin chops 1" thick
(about 10 ounces each)

Vegetable oil, for brushing

Salt and freshly ground pepper

## Method:

Preheat oven to 350 degrees.

Spread the pecans on a baking sheet and toast for 10 minutes, then chop.

In a small pan, combine maple syrup, vinegar, mustard, Sriracha and rosemary and bring to a boil. Simmer over moderate heat until reduced to ½ cup, about 10 minutes. Discard the rosemary.

Brush the pork chops with oil and season with salt and pepper. Grill over moderate heat, turning once, until lightly charred and nearly cooked through, about 10 minutes. Generously brush the maple glaze all over the chops and grill, turning once or twice, until lightly caramelized, another 2–3 minutes.

Transfer the pork chops to a platter, sprinkle with the pecans and serve.

# LOIN OF PORK STUFFED WITH FIGS, PROSCIUTTO AND SAGE

I recently decided to adapt a Jamie Oliver recipe for the main course for friends. In *Jamie's Italy*, he has a recipe for pork chops with sage, and he stuffs the pork with a heavenly flavored butter, which uses apricots, prosciutto, garlic and sage.

I realized, however, standing in the pantry frantically scouring shelves, that I had no apricots. This is only surprising because my mother-in-law once said, not unkindly, that heaven forbid there were to be an emergency and there was no food available, we could all quite happily live off the food in my pantry for a good year. This is not untrue. I have cans and cans, and jars and jars, and boxes and boxes. I seem to have this fear of running out, and heaven forbid there are no anchovies when you need them . . .

Because I am lazy, I did what I so often do—searched for a substitute, which is sometimes wonderful and sometimes beyond God-awful terrible. I used dried figs instead of dried apricots, and it was magnificent—I even, dare I admit it, preferred the figs to the original.

I also used dried sage instead of fresh. My friend the Artist had brought me a "smudge stick" to clear my house of bad energy after an unpleasant incident with an unwelcome visitor. I haven't gotten round to using the smudge stick, which now looks like it's been on a starvation diet for about six months, thanks to me throwing half into this dinner.

It was quick, it was easy, and it was impressive—always a good thing for a lazy gourmet like myself.

SERVES 4

**Ingredients:**

1 loin of pork, around 1½ pounds

½ stick butter

6 dried figs

4 slices prosciutto

1 clove of garlic

8 fresh sage leaves, or about 1 teaspoon if using dried, which is far more pungent

Salt and pepper

1 tablespoon Dijon mustard

2 tablespoons honey

Olive oil

**Method:**

Preheat oven to 450 degrees.

Cut a pocket along the length of the pork, almost going through to the other side, but being careful not to. Think of the Muppets, and you will get the idea.

In a food processor, pulse the butter, figs, prosciutto, garlic, sage and seasoning, until a paste.

Fill loin with paste, and wrap with string to keep it together. Mix mustard and honey together, covering meat.

Drizzle with oil, place in oven and immediately turn heat down to 375 degrees. Cook for 1 hour.

# DAILY BABY BACK RIBS

Every Christmas Eve, we decide to invite a handful of friends over for cocktails and hors d'oeuvres, and then, quite by mistake, we seem to have stumbled upon the unlikely decision to make ribs.

It started with my friend Glenn, the rib man, who one year borrowed a friend's smoker and made dozens of enormous racks of ribs, dripping with a syrupy glaze, that were delicious. The friend with the smoker disappeared, and I started to make the ribs myself, experimenting with different rubs and glazes, for I am not a huge fan of barbeque sauce.

Glenn came over last year with his magic rub, and told me to slow cook the pork, taking it out at the end and covering it with brown sugar, then putting it back in to melt the sugar deliciously over the pork.

It was delicious, but it was also unnervingly sweet, like eating dessert and dinner at the same time. Many days later, Glenn admitted he had forgotten it wasn't supposed to be brown sugar, but maple syrup.

I started experimenting, and this is the recipe my whole family has fallen in love with. It is also the food that I am ashamed to admit I eat on a weekly basis. I cook up huge batches, separate them, and have them at least twice a week.

SERVES 6

## Ingredients:

2 tablespoons onion powder

6 cloves garlic, crushed

½ tablespoon hot paprika

½ tablespoon salt

3 racks pork baby back ribs

½ cup maple syrup

## Method:

Preheat oven to 350 degrees.

Combine onion powder, garlic, paprika and salt. Divide into 3, and rub into ribs.

Cover with aluminum foil and cook for 3 hours.

Uncover and glaze ribs with maple syrup.

Cook for 45 minutes uncovered.

# SLOW-BRAISED ONION CHICKEN

When I cooked for my Unwell Friend, her mother called this Juicy Chicken. My children call it Breakfast Chicken because, rather like Chinese food, it is even better the next day, cold. When I make it, I make enough to feed a small army, and it lasts us for days.

This is my grandmother's recipe, changed and adapted over the years, made better (I think) with the addition of paprika and garlic. It is from the old country, and not the old country of England; it is an Eastern European dish where the odds and ends of the chicken, the meaty, tough, dark parts, were thrown in a pot and stewed, literally, for hours until the meat was falling off the bone.

I do use chicken on the bone, thighs and drumsticks because they have more flavor, but Beloved, the Rower and Twin A refuse to eat anything other than breast, so feel free to substitute some, if not all, for breast. I always make sure I throw a few in for them, and the juiciness of the dish keeps even the breast from getting dry. Also, if the only chicken thighs you can find have no bone, it will be absolutely fine. There is more than enough flavor from the onions.

Adding so many onions keeps the meat moist and incredibly sweet as the natural sugars in the onions caramelize down. Nobody believes that there is no oil whatsoever in the dish, that the chicken and onions combined create more than enough liquid. I think of this dish as being super-healthy, as well as delicious.

This is the kind of dish where the quantities can be as imprecise as you like. Add more chicken for more people, less for less, same with the onions. The real key is filling a pot with more onions than you thought humanly possible. If you do that, it will all turn out okay.

SERVES 6–8

## Ingredients:

**10 large yellow onions**

**8–12 chicken thighs**

**8–12 drumsticks**

**4–6 chicken breasts**

**Salt and pepper**

**2 tablespoons paprika**

**6 cloves garlic, smashed and chopped**

## Method:

Preheat oven to 300 degrees.

Slice the onions and place in large, heavy soup pot on high heat. Turn the onions over and over for around 10 minutes until they are starting to brown. Don't worry too much about burning, just keep turning.

Season chicken with salt, pepper and paprika and add to pot with garlic. Push the chicken pieces down so there is a layer of onion over them. Place in oven for 5 hours.

Serve the caramelized, juicy, delicious chicken the traditional way, with egg noodles and peas.

# MUM'S SPARE RIBS

I need to come clean. I am rubbish at barbeques. Great with anything on a stove, but when it comes to barbequeing, everything turns out black and charred. When we moved into this house, we needed a barbeque and didn't want to spend a fortune. We looked at Viking, looked at Weber, and decided instead of spending vast amounts so unnecessarily, we'd be really clever and investigate online.

We ended up finding a barbeque on Amazon that looked like the deal of the century—$1,200 reduced to about $200 and, best of all, I could "one-click" it! No filling in pesky details! No running downstairs to grab my credit card out of my purse! The grill looked amazing—big, silver and shiny, just like the very expensive Viking. We put it together (I do hate that everything these days arrives in kit form, as if all of us are experts at putting together furniture), congratulating ourselves on finding such a bargain.

And then we found its fatal flaw. You cannot control the heat. It has two temperatures. Burning, burning hot or . . . off. And, Beloved wants me to point out, it's entirely uneven. In other words, it may have cost only $200, but we may just as well have taken the $200 and thrown it down the toilet, and the reason it was reduced to $200 is because that's all it's worth.

Yesterday we had a barbeque for some neighbors. I dashed to Stew Leonard's, acknowledging I had to finally tackle a summer barbeque. I grabbed a few sides of baby backs and dashed home to make my mother's best rib marinade. I'm giving it to you, because it's delicious, but it wasn't so delicious last night. It works best when you marinate the meat for a couple of hours, then slow cook the ribs for a few hours, on a lowish heat (around 300 degrees), until the meat is falling off the bone.

It doesn't work so well, we discovered, when you are rushing around in a panic, don't marinate the meat at all, cook for an hour and then stick it on your super-hot-turn-everything-it-touches-into-charcoal barbeque at the end to give it that authentic barbeque flavor.

Basically, we sat down to coal.

Yum.

Back to my spare coal recipe. Don't cook it as I cooked it; cook it as my mother cooks it, and it will be delicious. Good luck!

# MUM'S SPARE RIBS

"Equal amounts" (this is how my mother writes down her recipes. I'm lucky the amounts were even in there. Often it's just the ingredients, which is all you need when you're that good a cook. Not there yet. Clearly.)

SERVES 6

### Ingredients:

½ cup ketchup

½ cup Worcestershire sauce

½ cup soy sauce

½ cup malt vinegar

½ cup brown sugar

2 racks spare ribs

### Method:

Preheat oven to 450 degrees.

Mix all ingredients and marinate meat for at least 1 hour.

Cover ribs with aluminum foil and turn oven down to 350 degrees. Cook for 2½–3 hours.

Uncover and either cook for a further 40 minutes or place on grill until crispy and stickily delicious.

# A.N.'S SLOW SHOULDER OF LAMB

I have no idea who A.N. is, but a piece of paper with this recipe scrawled on it in my mother's handwriting has been stuck in my recipe book for years. I love slow-cooked meat, especially lamb, and frequently make this with lamb shanks. I have also added anchovies because anchovies always bring out the taste of lamb, and no, you cannot taste the anchovies at all.

However, a word of warning: be careful to not only mince the anchovies very small, but also ensure they are evenly distributed. Last year, after I had surgery and had to be off my feet for two weeks, my parents flew over from London to help look after us, which mostly entailed cooking all day long for our enormous family.

My father, who is a very good cook, made his famous meatloaf, and all the Smalls crowed over it, except for Twin A, who confided with a frown that it was merely "okay" and tasted of fish.

Don't be ridiculous, I said. How could it taste of fish? My father—who is a big fan of experimentation because, frankly, who in their right mind would throw anchovies in meatloaf destined for children—then admitted he had thrown in some anchovies, had forgotten to mix them in, and they had all ended up in Twin A's slice.

SERVES 8

## Ingredients:

4 pound shoulder of lamb

Large can white beans, undrained

1 cup dry white wine

Large onion, roughly chopped

10 shallots, roughly chopped

6 tomatoes, quartered

3 tablespoons tomato purée

6 anchovies, finely chopped

Salt and pepper

10 cloves garlic, whole and peeled

2 bay leaves

3 sprigs rosemary

2 cups chicken stock

## Method:

Preheat oven to 275 degrees.

Put shoulder in good ovenware casserole with beans and liquid, the wine, onions, garlic, shallots, tomato purée and anchovies. Salt and pepper to taste. Tuck in bay leaves and rosemary and cover casserole dish.

Cook in oven for 4 hours, then increase temperature to 425 degrees for another hour or so.

Have a look to make sure it is not drying out.

You can substitute black olives for the anchovies, if preferred.

# FRUIT AND MINT STUFFED SHOULDER OF LAMB

The sweet and sour, the dried fruit and mint, always make me think of Lebanese food, which I love. Recently, a Lebanese restaurant opened up nearby, and I took the Smalls for their first foray. They were decidedly suspicious, until huge baskets of steaming freshly made pita bread started arriving, and soon all our meze, our small plates of assorted salads, and hot starters, disappeared. The waitress kept laughing at how much they were eating.

I didn't think they'd have room for the lamb we had ordered for the main course, but they did. As did I. This dish reminds me of that night. As with all my recipes, feel free to substitute, particularly the dried fruit. I have made this solely with prunes, but it is equally good made solely with figs or dates.

Also, 1 cup of cooked rice can be substituted for the pine nuts.

SERVES 4

## Ingredients:

2 tablespoons olive oil

1 small onion, finely chopped

2 cloves garlic, crushed

¼ cup slivered almonds

½ cup pine nuts

¼ cup prunes, chopped

⅛ cup dried figs, chopped

⅛ cup dates, chopped

Handful of mint leaves, chopped

Juice of ½ lime

Salt and pepper

1¾ pounds shoulder of lamb

## Method:

Preheat oven to 325 degrees.

Heat oil, sauté onion until soft. Add garlic, almonds, pine nuts and fruit, cook for 2 more minutes. Add mint, lime juice and seasoning, and mix well.

Cut a pocket in lamb and stuff, wrap tightly in foil, place in roasting tray and cook for 40 minutes.

Open foil, increase temperature to 400 degrees and cook for 15 minutes.

# SHEPHERD'S PIE

My freezer always, always has ground beef in it, and this is the quick, easy, can't-think-of-what-to-cook-for-the-kids supper. Technically, by the way, this is actually Cottage Pie, but everyone I know in America calls it Shepherd's Pie. For a true Shepherd's Pie, you would substitute minced lamb for the ground beef, but no one in America has ever heard of Cottage Pie, so I have taken artistic license.

Incidentally, I am not a huge fan of potatoes. Often, instead of mashed potatoes, I steam two heads of cauliflower, mash them with a dollop of sour cream and butter and use that instead. It is just a matter of taste, but the lightness of the cauliflower is something I have actually grown to prefer.

SERVES 4–6

## Ingredients:

1 tablespoon olive oil

1 large onion, finely diced

½ cup carrots, finely diced

¼ cup celery, finely diced

Salt and pepper

2 cups ground beef

½ teaspoon cinnamon

2 sprigs fresh thyme, finely chopped

1 tablespoon chopped flat-leaf parsley

1 tablespoon all-purpose flour

1¼ cups chicken stock

1 tablespoon tomato purée

Worcestershire sauce

2 pounds potatoes

¼ cup butter

¼ cup grated cheese

## Method:

Preheat oven to 400 degrees.

Heat ½ tablespoon oil in skillet, add onions and sauté for around 5 minutes, until slightly brown. Add carrot and celery. Cook 5 minutes, then remove from pan and set aside.

Turn up heat, add remaining oil, season beef well before adding, then cook, breaking up with spatula, until brown. Add onion mixture back into pan with cinnamon, thyme and parsley.

Stir in flour, then stock, tomato purée and a liberal sprinkling of Worcestershire sauce (to taste; I like tons). Turn heat down to low, cover, and cook gently for around half an hour.

While meat is cooking, peel potatoes, dice into even-sized rough cubes and add to a pan of cold water. Do not add salt as it breaks down the starch in the potatoes. Bring water to boil and simmer for around 25 minutes, or until potatoes are cooked.

Push potatoes through a ricer or mash with a hand masher, but do not use a blender or the potatoes will turn into a sticky mess. Add butter and salt and pepper.

Transfer meat to casserole dish, cover with potatoes, sprinkle cheese over the top. Bake for around half an hour or until top is golden.

# BRAISED SHORT RIBS WITH MARMALADE GLAZE

When I went to culinary school, I learned the secret to excellent braising, which involves searing meat in hot fat to brown, then slow cooking in liquid, covering about ⅔ of the meat, in a heavy pot until the meat is tender enough to fall apart with the gentlest of prods.

The secret involves parchment paper. Instead of covering the pot with a lid, which leaves a large gap between the food and the lid allowing all the flavor to evaporate while cooking, they taught us to make a parchment paper lid.

With my oval Le Creuset that I use for all braises, I cut the parchment, then roughly bend it over the empty pot to leave an imprint of the shape before cutting it out.

When the meat is ready to be covered, the parchment lid sits directly on top of the meat, essentially trapping all the flavor. It was the best thing I learned, apart from omelets, which I shall save for another time. It transforms dishes such as this.

SERVES 6

### Ingredients:

**12 beef short ribs**

**Salt and pepper**

**Olive oil (not extra-virgin), or vegetable oil**

**4 carrots, chopped**

**2 onions, chopped**

**2 stalks celery, chopped**

**4 sprigs fresh thyme**

**6 stalks of fresh parsley**

**1 teaspoon whole black peppercorns**

**1 bay leaf**

**2 cups chicken stock**

**1 can peeled tomatoes**

**1 teaspoon lemon juice**

#### Glaze:

**1 cup soy sauce**

**1 cup orange marmalade**

**1 cup orange juice**

**1 tablespoon minced garlic**

**1 teaspoon grated fresh ginger**

### Method:

Preheat oven to 350 degrees.

Whisk glaze ingredients in bowl. Add ribs and salt and pepper. Toss to coat. Cover and refrigerate at least 2 hours, preferably overnight.

Heat oil in Dutch oven until sizzling. Quickly brown ribs on all sides in small batches, ensuring ribs don't touch each other. Transfer to a plate.

Add carrots, onions and celery to same pan. Stir and scrape up all "sucs"—brown bits left by meat—for around 5 minutes, until vegetables are lightly browned.

Add thyme, parsley, peppercorns and bay leaf. Stir well.

Add ribs.

Add glaze, chicken stock and tomatoes.

Bring to a boil, then reduce to simmer. Cover and put in oven for 2 hours or until meat is very tender.

Remove ribs when cooked. Strain remaining sauce through fine sieve, bring to a boil then simmer until reduced. Add salt and pepper to sauce, and finish with lemon juice.

Serve with creamy polenta.

# FISH ESCABÈCHE

I often think that it is because I grew up in England, a child of parents who were born during the war, when food was rationed and everything was scarce, that I am so keen on leftovers.

I throw nothing away. Everything goes back in the fridge and is reconstituted somehow. When, days later, I am forced to throw away stale rice and sour food, it is always with a heavy heart. And nothing makes me happier than finding a recipe to reuse something I think I've had enough of.

Being English, we do occasionally give in to the craving for fish and chips, and being American, too, we always end up with enormous portions and half left over.

Which is how Fish Escabèche came about. I made a sweet and sour sauce, Filipino-style, with carrots, peppers and cucumbers and poured it over the fried fish to create an entirely new dish. The sauce would work equally well with chicken or thick eggplant slices, dredged in flour and lightly fried, for a vegetarian option.

SERVES 6

## Ingredients:

½ cup sugar

½ cup white vinegar

½ cup water

3 tablespoons tomato paste

1 carrot, peeled and cut into thin slices

1 green pepper, cut into thin strips

1 red pepper, cut into thin strips

1 cucumber, peeled and cut into thin slices

2 pounds leftover fried fish, or a white fish, cut into strips, dredged in flour, then egg, and lightly fried in oil for around 8 minutes on each side or until cooked

Bunch of cilantro, finely chopped

## Method:

Combine sugar, vinegar, water and tomato paste in pan.

Add carrot, cook on medium heat for around 5 minutes, then add peppers and cucumber.

Bring to boil and immediately turn down to simmer for a further 5 minutes.

Arrange fish on platter. Pour sauce all over and garnish with cilantro.

Serve with white rice.

# TUNA WITH CILANTRO LIME SAUCE AND GUACAMOLE

My eldest son discovered his passion—rowing—at around the same time he shot up to 6' 5", most of which is legs. This makes him an excellent rower, and every day he takes the bus straight to the rowing club, kills himself with exercise for three hours, then comes home, ready to eat a horse.

Some of the time, I serve him food that disappoints. Today, he came home, with the daughter—Junior Rower—both of them charging through the house announcing they were starving.

I served them this, because even though it is cold and rainy, and I am completely fed up with winter extending far beyond its natural course, I am determined to pretend it's spring. I am wearing the brightest of colors and cooking the kinds of food that make me think of summer evenings sitting around a big teak table on the terrace, with my favorite people.

Their eyes lit up at the sight of the lushness of the green avocado heaped on top of the seared tuna, jewels of tomato glistening brightly, and their first bite sent both of them into dreamy raptures. "This," declared the Rower, his eyes shut in bliss, as Junior Rower munched happily beside him, "is happy food."

Indeed.

SERVES 4

## Ingredients:

4 tuna steaks

Salt and pepper

2 handfuls of cilantro leaves, chopped and stems removed

1 teaspoon grated fresh ginger

1 clove garlic, minced

Juice and zest from 1 lime

1 tablespoon soy sauce

1 teaspoon sugar

2 tablespoons olive oil

## Simple Guacamole:

1 avocado, mashed

1 tomato, finely diced

Juice of ¼ lime

Sprinkling of hot sauce or hot chili pepper

Salt

## Method:

Sprinkle both sides of tuna steaks with salt and pepper. Combine cilantro, ginger, garlic, lime juice, zest, soy sauce, sugar and olive oil. Add tuna steaks and let marinate for at least 2 hours, preferably overnight.

Remove tuna from the marinade and grill for 3–5 minutes per side. Pour the marinade into a small pot and reduce on high heat until mixture has thickened.

Combine all guacamole ingredients.

When ready to serve, pour the sauce over tuna and add a spoonful of guacamole on top.

# FISH BALLS

I quite often make fish cakes, even though the Smalls are extremely undecided about fish, unless it comes battered and fried, with chips on the side (English version of chips, i.e., fries).

The other day I decided to make fish balls instead, which my grandmother used to make from scratch in London. I googled a few recipes as I wanted to use a white fish rather than my usual fish cakes of either tuna or salmon, and I had no idea how they would turn out.

It was a major winner. They are so *completely* delicious, I urge you to try them.

I had them cooling on the counter and the Smalls went bananas. I didn't, obviously, tell them they were fish balls. I just said nothing. Mention the "f" word, and I think they would have gone running, but as it was, they recognized it was something fried, ergo, unhealthy, and proceeded to swipe about half of them.

(Even the Maniac, who for years ate nothing but pasta and cheese.)

SERVES 4

### Ingredients:

1½ pounds haddock fillet skinned

1½ pounds cod fillet skinned

1½ medium onions

3 eggs

3 teaspoons salt

Pinch of white pepper

1 tablespoon oil, plus more for frying

½–1 cup bread crumbs

3 tablespoons sugar

### Method:

Peel and roughly chop onion. Put into food processor with the eggs, seasoning and oil. Process until mixture is a smooth paste. Set aside.

Cut fish into 1" chunks and put half into the food processor. Process for 5 seconds until the fish is finely chopped. Then process second half.

Add to onion paste with bread crumbs and sugar, and mix well. (You may need more sugar—you want it to taste slightly sweet and salty in equal measure.) It should be firm enough to shape into a loose ball about the size of a medium-sized meatball.

If not firm enough, add a little more of the bread crumbs. If too firm, add a little water.

Add enough oil (about 1" deep) to a frying pan and heat until sizzling. Carefully lower fish balls into oil and fry, turning often, until they are golden brown all over. Remove when cooked and drain on paper towel.

Can be served hot or left to cool.

# KEDGEREE

Kedgeree is a Victorian breakfast dish that I have now adopted as a modern brunch or supper dish, and every time I make it people go nuts. Even my children get excited when they smell the onions softening in curried butter; they love this dish.

In England, we make it with smoked haddock, poaching the haddock and using the liquid to cook the rice. I haven't yet been able to find smoked haddock in America and had to get creative to find the unique flavor of kedgeree. Fish sauce and presmoked filets of salmon work wonders.

SERVES 4

### Ingredients:

½ cup (1 stick) butter

1 onion, finely diced

1 teaspoon curry powder

1 cup rice

2 cups water

1 teaspoon fish sauce

1½ cups smoked trout filets

3 hard-boiled eggs, chopped

3 heaping tablespoons chopped flat-leaf parsley

1 tablespoon lemon juice

Salt and pepper

### Method:

Melt ¼ cup butter in skillet. Soften onion in it for 5 minutes.

Stir curry powder into onion, stir in rice and add water and fish sauce.

Stir well, bring to boil, cover and turn down to a gentle simmer for 15 minutes, or until rice is cooked.

Remove smoked trout flesh from skin. Flake. Add to cooked rice with eggs, parsley, lemon juice, and remaining butter. Cover pan and replace on gentle heat for 5 minutes before serving. Add seasoning to taste.

# ASIAN STEAMED CLEAR BASS

This is one of those almost stupidly easy dishes that doesn't sound the slightest bit interesting (by now you may have already turned the page), but if there were only one recipe in this book you had to cook, this would be it.

I remember reading this recipe (thank you, Mum!), and thinking, *Well. That sounds boring.* But something, perhaps a smidgen of common sense, prevailed, and I did make this dish one night for friends. As we all took that first bite, all of our eyes widened at the sheer deliciousness of this fish.

The salt and sugar create the perfect blend of sweet and sour. This is truly better than anything I have ever eaten in a Chinese restaurant, and Chinese food is my all-time favorite food.

Serve it simply, with steamed white rice. I have a friend who ate it our house, declared it the best thing he'd ever eaten, then went off home and, because he loves cooking and needs to make things his own, adapted it, adding all kinds of things like sesame oil, fish sauce and various spices. It needs nothing other than the list of ingredients below.

SERVES 4

### Ingredients:

2 pounds sea bass (preferably one fish if you can get it)

½ teaspoon salt

½ teaspoon sugar

1″ piece of fresh ginger, peeled and julienned

8 scallions, finely julienned in 2″ lengths, green and white parts separated

6 tablespoons groundnut or corn oil

4 tablespoons soy sauce

### Method:

Rinse the fish and pat dry. Make 2–3 diagonal slashes on both sides of the fish.

Steam in a fish poacher or steamer over high heat for about 8 minutes, or until the fish is cooked and flakes easily.

Remove the cover, turn the heat off and carefully place the fish on a serving platter and sprinkle with the salt and sugar.

Spread the ginger over the fish, then the green part of the scallions, followed by the white part.

Heat the oil in a small pan over high heat until smoking. Pour it little by little over the scallions and ginger, which will sizzle and cook as the oil hits them.

Finish by drizzling soy sauce over the entire fish. Serve with fragrant white rice.

## SALMON (PREFERABLY NOT FROM THE MAN WITH THE VAN) PARCELS WITH WATERCRESS, ARUGULA AND CREAM CHEESE

Last weekend the doorbell rang on Sunday afternoon, and I opened the door to find a very nice man with a van selling what he said was organic meats and fish.

I like to think of myself as a savvy city chick, and I was about to say thanks but no thanks, but the van looked professional, and he was a great salesman. So when he said he was just on the way back from dropping off at the neighbors—he didn't say which neighbors specifically— I said, okay. I'll try it.

He also invoked the name of the local grocery store owner, although given that the owner has access to his own fantastic quality meat and fish, I think, in hindsight, it's extremely unlikely he'd be buying from the man with the van (although I'd quite like to track him down and find out).

The man with the van piled box after box after box on our driveway. Filet mignon, rib steak, chicken kebabs, king crab legs, crab cakes and so on and so forth.

I cooked the filet mignon that night. "Darling," I called Beloved over. "Does that look okay to you?"

"Hmmm." We both stood peering at the meat, which was distinctly gray. "Is it *supposed* to be that grayish color?"

"I don't know," I said. I then threw the rib steaks on for the Smalls.

"Darling." Beloved called me over. "Have you ever seen fat that color before?"

The fat was a bright, luminous yellow.

"Er . . . no."

Research seems to indicate that when the fat is yellow, it is often because the meat has been derived from an older animal. These animals clearly weren't just old, they were *ancient*. I think they might have had the longevity gene.

We then unwrapped the tuna. "Sushi quality Ahi tuna," said the man with the van. It was very pink. So pink it looked like it had crawled out of the ocean about 10 seconds prior. Highly suspiciously, unnaturally pink. And it smelled fishy. In more ways than one.

We checked the label to find it had, as Beloved suspected, been treated with CO. This is a practice where tuna is sprayed with carbon monoxide to turn it pink. The problem is, it preserves only the color, not the quality, so there's no way to tell how old the fish is. Put it like this: you could keep the tuna in an overheated hall closet for a year and it would still be pink.

In other words, there is no way to tell if the fish is spoiled. Unless you smell it.

And this didn't smell so good.

I have the man with the van's brochure, but suffice it to say, I shall not be calling him again. If a charming salesman knocks on your door and offers you frozen food from his van, I'd invite him in to cook up (and eat) a steak first before committing. However, the crab cakes were good.

I leave you with one of my mother's new super-easy and super-impressive recipes.

# SALMON PARCELS WITH WATERCRESS, ARUGULA AND CREAM CHEESE

SERVES 4

## Ingredients:

1 bag watercress

1 bag arugula

1 bag spinach

1 (8 oz) package cream cheese

Zest of 1 lemon

Salt and pepper

1 sheet frozen puff pastry, thawed

4 salmon filets

1 egg, beaten with
1 tablespoon milk

## Method:

Preheat oven to 350 degrees.

Blend the watercress, arugula and spinach in a food processor until finely chopped.

Add cream cheese, lemon zest and seasoning and pulse until blended.

Put ½ to one side to serve alongside salmon parcels.

Roll out pastry and cut into 4 squares.

Place salmon in middle, season and spread ¼ of the cream cheese mixture over the top. Pull corners of pastry over fish and seal at top. Brush with egg wash. Do this 4 times.

Cook for around 25 minutes, or until pastry is golden.

Serve with rest of cream cheese mixture and a green salad.

# WHITE FISH PESTO SANDWICHES

Every year, we go and stay with my parents on a small island in the Bahamas, which has the most beautiful beaches I have ever seen, and the most terrible food I have ever eaten, anywhere.

I know, I know. You don't believe me. You probably think, as I once did, that the food would be fresh fish, fresh lobster, delicious fruits. But everywhere you go, it is club sandwiches on thin white bread with processed cheese and ham, frozen lobster and recently, at lunch, we sent back the chicken on our salad because it was raw.

Beloved and the Brother went out one morning, banging their chests and hollering about catching dinner. They went spear-lobstering (my own title) and caught two little lobsters. *Very* little. They might make a couple of hors d'oeuvres. If we were lucky. The boys spent the entire morning discussing how to cook them.

Later that day, we set off to the Beach Club for dinner, then to a friend's for drinks, then to the local bar, for—what else—many more drinks. This year, on New Year's Eve in the Bahamas, I was determined to be up at midnight. Last year, on a cruise, I went to bed early with depression. I had long suspected I was not a cruise sort of person. The cruise confirmed it.

Our island in the Bahamas is never going to be a destination for the Glitterati, simply because if you want to eat good food, you have to cook it at home. My parents cooked an amazing dinner one night, which I watched from my vantage point of lying on a sofa under a blanket, unable to move, worryingly, I suspected, due to the raw chicken at lunch. By the next day, I was much better, well enough to taste leftovers of my mother's white fish pesto sandwich, and a warm chocolate and banana cake that was to die for.

The fish is wonderful. I can't say it's the perfect dish for the Bahamas, but compared to raw chicken salad, it's pretty damn good.

SERVES 4

## Ingredients:

2 cartons cherry tomatoes

¼ cup sun-dried tomatoes

4 cloves garlic, sliced

¼ cup black olives, pitted and halved

Dried red pepper flakes

Salt and pepper

Olive oil

4 filets white fish (tilapia or cod)

½ cup Basil Lemon Pesto (see page 18)

8 ounces prosciutto

## Method:

Preheat oven to 350 degrees.

Mix cherry tomatoes, sun-dried tomatoes, garlic and olives together. Add chili flakes to taste, salt and pepper and a generous dousing of olive oil. Roast for around 30 minutes, until tomatoes are turning brown and wrinkled.

Sandwich two filets of fish with ¼ cup pesto each, and season with salt and pepper. Wrap each sandwich with prosciutto, tucking in the ends. Place fish on partly roasted tomatoes and continue to cook, uncovered, for a further 20–25 minutes.

# MILD GREEN FISH CURRY

I already mentioned my disaster with the green curry when I chopped up three thousand super-hot chilies and wondered why I could barely get close to the blender, the heat was so strong.

Luckily, it didn't put me off green curries for life, although it should have. I do have a penchant for spicy food, but, unsurprisingly, not when it comes to green curries. Then I'd much rather they were flavorful, but mild.

We are exceptionally lucky in having a wonderful, but tiny, Thai restaurant almost on our doorstep. I seem to have a habit of living near wonderful Thai restaurants. My very first apartment in London was in the basement of an old Georgian terraced house in Pimlico, opposite a Thai restaurant. It was my savior many, many times when I got home after a long day at work, scooting over the road for a quick bite to eat, and it left me with a lingering love of lemongrass.

SERVES 4

### Ingredients:

Groundnut oil

1 large onion

2 cloves garlic

Handful of cilantro

6 scallions

½ teaspoon sugar

3 stalks lemongrass, bruised

Zest of 1 lime

1 can coconut milk

1 cup frozen peas

1½ pounds firm fish (salmon, cod, shrimp)

2 tablespoons fish sauce

Juice of 1 lime

### Method:

Heat oil in a skillet and add onion. Soften until starting to go transparent, then add garlic and cook for 1 more minute.

Transfer to blender, with the cilantro and scallions. Blend with sugar.

Transfer back to pan, add lemongrass stalks and lime zest. Add coconut milk. Bring to high heat, then turn down to simmer for 15 minutes.

Add peas and fish. Continue cooking until fish is cooked through, 6–8 minutes.

At last minute, add fish sauce and lime juice.

# SHRIMP CAKES

I once went for a walk along the beach with the Smalls, where we stumbled upon thousands of mussels on the rocks at low tide, just waiting to be harvested and steamed in garlic and white wine. What was a girl to do other than stop a passing dog walker, request a spare blue plastic bag normally used for other things and fill said bag, and all pockets, with mussels?

The children were thrilled at the free food we were gathering and cooking ourselves, and the mussels were among the best I have ever had.

Other than mussels, and the occasional smoked salmon, the other fish they really look forward to is shrimp. Heaven forbid we put out a shrimp platter for a cocktail party if the Smalls are home. Within 10 short minutes, it is demolished. These shrimp cakes satisfy them in every way and, best of all, there is no flour necessary to bind them together.

I have no idea why shrimp sticks together so willingly, but I am very happy it does.

SERVES 4

### Ingredients:

2 tablespoons chopped cilantro

1 pound raw shrimp, roughly chopped

¼ cup coconut milk

Minced jalapeño or Thai pepper

6 scallions

1" piece of ginger, peeled and grated

Coconut oil to sauté

### Dipping Sauce:

2 tablespoons chopped cilantro

1 clove garlic, minced

Salt and pepper

½ cup crème fraiche or sour cream

### Method:

Pulse cilantro, shrimp, coconut milk, jalapeño, scallions and ginger until combined but still chunky.

Form into balls and flatten about halfway with your palms. Sauté in melted coconut oil about 3 minutes on each side.

To make dipping sauce, combine cilantro, garlic, salt and pepper with crème fraiche or sour cream.

# WILD MUSHROOM POLENTA

I made this for Hugh Grant when I ended up cooking lunch for him rather than conducting our planned interview. I didn't know, at the time, that the only food he really loves are curries, which is a shame only because my brain is nothing if not *filled* with excellent curry recipes. But I made this instead, and the stuffed loin of pork, and he seemed delighted with the result.

I was pretty delighted with the result myself. Polenta always reminds me of sophisticated baby food, and there is nothing in the world I love more than baby food—I could live quite happily on apple sauce and Jell-O. The addition of the mushrooms and a drizzle of truffle oil makes it completely sublime.

SERVES 4

## Ingredients:

3 cups chicken stock

½ cup heavy cream

Salt and pepper

2 cups polenta

¼ cup mascarpone

4 tablespoons butter

½ cup parmesan cheese, grated

## Mushroom Sauce:

1 cup assorted gourmet mushrooms (porcini, morels, etc.)

1 clove garlic, minced

1 onion, finely chopped

2 tablespoons olive oil

1 sprig thyme

Salt and pepper

4 tablespoons chicken stock

Chopped flat-leaf parsley

Truffle oil to garnish (optional)

## Method:

Combine the stock, cream, salt and pepper and bring to a simmer. Add the polenta in a slow steady stream and bring the mixture back to a simmer. Stir with a wooden spoon and cook on a very low heat for 1 hour, stirring frequently. If the mixture begins to thicken too much, add more simmering stock. Finish with mascarpone and butter, then season and add the cheese. It should be like loose mashed potatoes.

To make the sauce, rinse the mushrooms thoroughly if fresh, then slice them and sauté them with garlic and onion in the oil for about 10 minutes. Add the thyme, salt, pepper and stock and turn the heat to high to reduce and thicken the sauce.

When ready to serve, spoon the sauce over the polenta, sprinkle with parsley and drizzle with truffle oil.

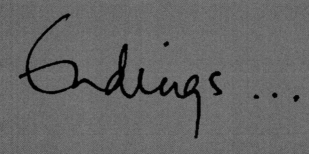

# Endings . . .

Sugar is my drug of choice. When I'm hungry, angry, lonely or tired, the first place I turn is sugar. The main course is usually only a means to get to the sugar, so desserts, as you can tell, are very important to me.

I don't do desserts very often and not for regular old family cooking, but when guests are coming over, there really is nothing like bringing out a homemade dessert. However wonderful our local bakers, and they are wonderful, you cannot taste the love baked into the food in the way you can with a home-cooked dessert.

I would far rather you brought me a cracked, broken, mushy pie that has been cooked in your own kitchen than a perfect one in a box bought from the local market. And if you can't make pies, buy some meringues, whip some cream and mix them together with strawberries for Eton Mess—you don't even need to make the strawberry coulis. There is something about food that has been prepared by someone you know that always makes it more delicious.

I am not a keen baker and have no patience for the science of baking. My friend, the Baker, pores over recipes, takes her time, follows every instruction to the letter. I am far too imprecise and impatient to do that, which is why the recipes collected here do not require that kind of attention and always, always turn out well.

# WARM CHOCOLATE AND BANANA CAKE

This is a Mum special. Which means she had scribbled the following on a piece of paper: choc, butter, sugar, 3 eggs, just over 8 oz flour, bit of baking p., 2 T cocoa p., 3 bananas. *And that was it.*

My mother's entire cookbook is like that. It needs an expert spy to crack her codes, because most of the recipes are a thousand years old, and she has long forgotten both the quantities and how to make the damned thing.

But warm banana and chocolate cake? This was worth getting to the bottom of, surely. I pressed her for information, she dredged up a few quantities from her memory, then talked me through the process.

Know that the longer you cream together butter and sugar (this is a rule with all cakes), the fluffier and lighter the cake will be.

This is very worth it. The chef on *Good Morning America* made this cake when I was on the show to talk about *Promises to Keep*, and Robin Roberts got up to do the next interview, then dashed back to the table to eat more cake. That's how good it is.

SERVES 8

Ingredients:

1 cup plain chocolate

1 cup unsalted butter, softened

1 cup sugar

3 eggs, beaten

1 cup plus 2 tablespoons flour

1 teaspoon baking powder

2 tablespoons cocoa powder

3 ripe bananas, mashed

Confectioners' sugar, for dusting

Method:

Preheat oven to 350 degrees.

Melt chocolate over a bain-marie, or use my lazy way of melting it *very*, *very* slowly in a microwave (otherwise it burns). In a ceramic bowl, microwave in 20-second intervals, each time stirring with a plastic spatula until smooth.

Cream together butter and sugar until pale (around 10 minutes).

Add eggs gradually, while beating.

Stir dry ingredients together in a bowl and fold into wet mix.

Add mashed banana and melted chocolate. Mix well.

Bake 45 minutes.

Cool and sprinkle with confectioners' sugar.

# LEMON AND ALMOND CAKE TART

One of my most favorite people in the world is my sister-in-law, Fishy. I was already living in the States when she became my sister-in-law, which is unfortunate on two levels. First, I don't get to see her nearly as often as I would like, and second, I don't get to experience her cooking.

My parents are always going over there for dinner and reporting back about delicious roast chickens and fantastic lamb. She is *the* expert at delicious, traditional, effortless comfort food and one of her best dishes, according to my mother, is her lemon and almond tart.

There really is nothing better than lemon and almond tart, particularly this one that is so densely citrusy, thanks to the puréed lemon. The almond extract and thick, moist texture makes it almost taste like marzipan, and the entire tart is heavenly.

SERVES 8

### Ingredients:

Butter for baking dish

1⅓ cups almond flour

1 teaspoon almond extract

8 tablespoons sugar

4 large eggs, separated

1 lemon, boiled in water for 20 minutes, seeds removed, then puréed to mash

Pinch of salt

½ cup confectioners' sugar

½ cup toasted slivered almonds

### Method:

Preheat oven to 375 degrees.

Butter a 9" tart pan and line with waxed paper.

In a food processor, combine almond flour and 6 tablespoons sugar.

Separately combine egg yolks, 2 tablespoons sugar, lemon purée and salt, and beat until smooth and pale. Add almond mixture and combine.

Beat egg whites to soft peaks, add confectioners' sugar, and combine. Beat 1 large spoonful of egg whites into almond mixture, then fold rest of almond mixture into egg whites.

Transfer to tart pan and bake for 35 minutes.

Dust with confectioners' sugar sprinkled through a sieve and cover top with toasted slivered almonds before serving.

# PUMPKIN GINGERBREAD TRIFLE

My mother-in-law, aka the Sherpa, gave this recipe to me. It was the start of my real bonding with the man who was to become my husband. We were on very polite, early dating behavior when we both offered to help clear the table after this insane dessert had been served. Within 30 seconds, the pair of us were hiding in the kitchen, spoon-deep in the crystal bowl, finishing this off. I knew then it was true love.

The first thing the Sherpa does is make gingerbread, which frankly, seems to me to be absolutely bonkers. The Sherpa is a wonderful cook, but she and I cook very differently. She likes fine French food, and I like throwing things together, very easily, and eating family-style. We threw a dinner party for her last year, and I asked, casually, whether she had any recipes she might like us to cook. "Oh yes," she said, her face lighting up. "I'll bring them over tomorrow."

The next day she appeared with a sheath of papers.

It was about 3" thick.

Apparently, while I was reading it, all the color drained from my face.

The Sherpa makes this trifle entirely from scratch. I would strongly advise a gingerbread mix, adding the fresh and crystallized ginger to give it some zing.

If, however, you are like the Sherpa and you still want to do it from scratch, even though I will think you are nuts, I have included the recipe for the gingerbread.

SERVES 8–10

**Ingredients for Gingerbread:**

Butter for baking dish
3 cups all-purpose flour
1 tablespoon ground cinnamon
1½ teaspoons ground cloves
1 teaspoon ground ginger
2 teaspoons baking soda
¾ teaspoon salt
1½ cups white sugar
1 cup vegetable oil
½ cup apple juice
1 cup dark molasses
2 eggs
1 tablespoon grated fresh ginger
½ cup chopped crystallized ginger

Method:

Preheat oven to 350 degrees.

Butter and flour a 10" springform pan.

Stir together flour, cinnamon, cloves, ground ginger, baking soda and salt in a bowl.

Mix sugar with oil, juice, molasses, eggs and fresh ginger in a large bowl. Mix in crystallized ginger. Stir in flour mixture.

Pour into prepared pan. Then bake for 1 hour.

Cool for 10 minutes, then remove from the pan and cool completely.

# PUMPKIN GINGERBREAD TRIFLE

**Pumpkin Custard:**

3 cups half-and-half

6 large eggs

½ cup granulated sugar

½ cup brown sugar, packed

⅓ cup molasses

1½ teaspoons ground cinnamon

1 teaspoon ground ginger

1 teaspoon ground nutmeg

⅛ teaspoon ground cloves

½ teaspoon salt

3 cups puréed pumpkin, or about 1½ cans


**Whipped Cream:**

1 quart heavy cream

½ teaspoon vanilla extract

¼ cup crystallized ginger


Method:

Preheat an oven to 325 degrees.

Scald the half-and-half in a heavy saucepan (which means take it to the edge of boiling, then remove from heat).

Beat eggs, sugar, molasses, cinnamon, ginger, nutmeg and salt. Mix in pumpkin and half-and-half. When it is smooth, put it in buttered baking dish, which you then put into a bain-marie: put dish into larger baking dish, and fill larger dish with hot water to about 1" below the rim of the custard dish. Bake for 50 minutes and start to check it. You want a set, firm custard, so that a knife inserted into the center comes out clean. Cool and refrigerate overnight.

To make whipped cream, whip heavy cream with vanilla extract, then fold in crystallized ginger, and set aside.

To assemble your trifle, spoon half the pumpkin custard into a trifle bowl and layer half the gingerbread over that and then half the whipped cream. Do it again. Top the final layer of whipped cream with gingersnaps, or gingersnap crumbs, and, if you like, drizzle with Calvados.

# SALTED CHOCOLATE MOUSSE

Chocolate mousse was the go-to dessert in my childhood home forever. I hadn't had it for years and years after I moved to America, but when I was at culinary school, we spent an afternoon on chocolate mousse. It was extremely fiddly, involved far more ingredients than I had ever used making it with my mum, and had a frightening amount of whipped cream. It was also completely delicious, but I have to be honest, I love my regular chocolate mousse, which requires nothing other than eggs and chocolate. I have only added the salt because salted chocolate is so delicious, so in right now and, therefore, so easy to find.

You can either use salted chocolate bars as the chocolate or regular semisweet chocolate, sprinkling sea salt on top. This is the easiest recipe in the whole wide world, as long as you follow the steps and make sure there is absolutely no yolk anywhere near the separated whites.

Top tip: Separate each egg individually before adding the whites to a large bowl. That way, if yolk gets in the white you have just broken, you only lose one egg rather than the entire batch.

SERVES 8

**Ingredients:**

**1 cup (8 ounces) good-quality salted chocolate or semisweet chocolate**

**6 eggs, separated**

**Pinch of salt (only if you are using semisweet chocolate)**

**Sea salt or shaved chocolate to garnish (optional)**

Method:

Separate the whites and the yolks, being extremely careful not to break the yolks into the whites.

Break up the chocolate and melt over a bain-marie, or microwave very slowly (see page 124). Set aside for 10 minutes.

Whisk the yolks until smooth. Stir in to slightly cooled chocolate until completely blended. Set aside.

Whisk whites until they are so thick, you are able to turn the bowl upside down and the whites stay exactly as they are. Take one large spoonful of the whites and whisk it into the chocolate mixture to lighten it.

Gradually fold chocolate mixture into the egg whites until fully combined. If you are using semisweet chocolate, add a pinch of salt as you mix. When the color is evenly chocolaty throughout, transfer to a glass bowl, or individual glasses if you are using.

Set in fridge for at least 1 hour. Garnish with shaved chocolate (and a pinch of sea salt if you used semisweet chocolate).

# ALMOST FLOURLESS ORANGE CAKE
# WITH MARMALADE GLAZE

I don't *get* cake. Unless it is as damp and squidgy as waterlogged sand. Dry and fluffy does not float my boat, but this orange cake, both heavy and delicate at the same time, is something I adore.

I have been known to eat every bit of frosting, icing and cream filling on an entire cake, leaving just the cake behind. I have also been known to bring back huge tubs of ice cream and fish through them for every bit of cookie dough, crunch and toffee, leaving half a tub of ice cream soup.

With this cake, I now either cook the orange in water or take the lazy option of nuking it in the microwave, then removing the seeds and blending the entire thing to a pulp. I have learned to do this with all cakes that call for lemons and oranges. It lends the most intense citrus taste, far more than squeezing out the juice and zesting the fruit, and it gives you a moist, lovely cake.

# ALMOST FLOURLESS ORANGE CAKE WITH MARMALADE GLAZE

SERVES 8

## Ingredients:

1 orange

3 eggs

1 cup confectioners' sugar

¼ cup sifted flour

1 teaspoon baking powder

3 cups ground almonds

½ cup orange marmalade

Icing sugar for dusting

Small carton whipping cream (optional)

Rind of 1 orange (optional)

## Method:

Preheat oven to 350 degrees.

Grease an 8" springform cake tin and line it with greaseproof paper.

Put the orange in a pan, cover with water and simmer for 1 hour (or nuke in a microwave for around 25 minutes) until soft. Cut the orange in half, remove seeds and purée in a food processor.

Beat the eggs and sugar until pale and thick. Fold in the flour, baking powder, almonds and orange purée. Pour into the tin and bake for 1 hour.

Melt the marmalade in a small pan, then pour through a fine sieve, pressing to get all the juice out. Spread the rind-free juice over the cake.

When cool, sift the icing sugar over the cake. Mix whipped cream with the orange rind and serve alongside.

# PAVLOVA

I just read an article about a woman who, I believe, has written a book about her attempts to date by taking homemade cakes into bars and serving them to single men. It sounded like a wonderful year, her year of cake-making and flirting. However, it seemed that by the end of year, despite all the confidence she had learned and the great experiences she had had, she was still resolutely single.

I am certain that's because she didn't make Pavlova.

If you happen to be a single woman in search of a good man, look no further than this recipe. Every good man I know sighs with delight over the prospect of meringue and whipped cream, and I am quite sure that the two men, aside from husband and family, who love me most in the world do so because of my Pavlova.

It's a frothy confection of meringue, whipped cream and fresh fruit, created in Australia in the 1920s to honor the arrival of the famed Russian ballet dancer Anna Pavlova.

The outside of the meringue should be lightly browned, and the inside chewy and sweet, almost like marshmallow. Don't worry about cracks in the meringue—pile on the whipped cream and fruit to hide, and make sure you use sugar.

A side story: a couple of years ago, we wandered over to Greenwich for a book party for the Countess Cristina de Vogüé who had written a sumptuous book called *Decadent Desserts*. Tall, ridiculously elegant, with dramatic makeup and swept-back hair, a permanent cigarette in a long, thin cigarette holder and a throaty French accent, the Countess was mesmerizing. She stood and told the story of this book, which contains her own story of how she came to be Lady of Château Vaux-le-Vicomte, 30 miles outside of Paris.

She told of her mistakes, of the time their restaurant hosted a party from IBM, and they had requested strawberry meringues. Making them in advance, she asked the chef how to ensure the meringues would stay stiff. "Use lots and lots of sugar," he advised.

She did, whipping the egg whites and sugar into a frenzy, relieved that they came out just as perfectly as the chef had said.

At the end of the evening the representative from IBM asked to see her. "Why is it," he asked, "that the meringues are so salty?"

Whoops.

# PAVLOVA

SERVES 8–10

## Ingredients:

4 egg whites, room temperature

1 cup confectioners' sugar

½ tablespoon cornstarch

1 teaspoon vanilla extract

1 teaspoon white vinegar

½ cup heavy cream

Fresh fruit and/or berries (e.g., strawberries cut up, raspberries, kiwi fruit)

1 tablespoon lemon juice

## Method:

Preheat oven to 275 degrees.

Whisk the egg whites in a squeaky-clean bowl until soft peaks form. Add the sugar while whisking, a spoonful at a time, and keep whisking until the peaks are glossy and stiff.

Sprinkle cornstarch, ½ teaspoon vanilla, lemon juice, and vinegar and fold in.

Spread the meringue on an oiled baking sheet or a Silpat in a circular shape. Make a slight well in the middle.

Bake the meringue for around 1 hour and 15 minutes, until a pale eggshell color.

Turn oven off, but DO NOT REMOVE MERINGUE! Crack the oven door to allow the meringue to cool in the oven. Expect cracks.

Remove meringue before serving.

Whip cream with remaining vanilla until peaks form.

Spread cream over cool meringue, and cover with fresh fruit.

# CHESS TART

Once upon a time, we were at Martha Stewart's house when she pulled a rather plain-looking tart from the fridge and cut us a generous slice. I thought it was perhaps some sort of meringue, put the first forkful in my mouth, and if I had died at that moment, I would have died happy.

Her recipe for Chess Tart is exquisite and calls for a crust of crushed Nilla Wafers. If you have them, you will need around 45, crushed with 5 tablespoons of melted butter, 2 tablespoons of sugar, and ¼ tablespoon of salt.

I don't often have Nilla Wafers in the house, but I do always have the rest of the ingredients, and so I often make this with a classic pie crust. You can buy frozen pie crust and use that, but honestly, it is such an easy pastry to make, and takes seconds, I don't know why you wouldn't make this.

Know that of everything in this book, this is the most extraordinary tart you will ever taste in your life. It is the dessert the children request whenever we have a party. It tastes like a chewy, caramel, sugary, yummy, delicious sin. As you will see from the ingredients, it is indeed sinful, but for special occasions, so very worth it.

Do not, under any circumstances, eat this before a wedding. Or a big party. Or anything that requires you to squeeze into a dress that almost, almost fits.

# CHESS TART

SERVES 8–10

## Ingredients for Pie Crust:

2½ cups all-purpose flour

1 teaspoon sugar

1 teaspoon salt

1 cup (2 sticks) cold butter, diced

¼–½ cup ice cold water

## Method for Pie Crust:

Preheat oven to 425 degrees.

To make pastry: combine flour, sugar and salt in large bowl. Put in a food processor with butter and pulse until it is like damp sand. As processor runs, slowly drizzle ice water just until dough holds together. No more than 30 seconds. Don't add too much! When it comes together into a ball, wrap in plastic wrap and chill for around 1 hour before use.

When ready, coat a 9" fluted tart pan with removable bottom with cooking spray. Put parchment paper on the bottom. Roll out dough on floured surface to cover pan. Press gently into edges and sides. Trim. Line with foil, fill with dried beans and bake 5 minutes. Remove foil and beans and bake a further 2–3 minutes until golden.

Let cool slightly.

## Ingredients for Filling:

1 cup white sugar

½ cup brown sugar

1 tablespoon cornmeal

Salt

3 eggs

1 egg yolk

1 teaspoon vanilla extract

½ cup (1 stick) butter, melted

## Method for Filling:

Reduce oven to 325 degrees.

Mix together sugars, cornmeal and salt, breaking up clumps. Whisk in eggs, yolk and vanilla. Whisk in butter.

Pour filling into tart shell. Bake until top is dark golden brown and edge is set but center is still a bit wobbly, 35–40 minutes.

Transfer pan to a wire rack and let cool for 15 minutes. Refrigerate until cooled, at least 2 hours or overnight.

# PLUM TARTE TATIN

Cooking lunch for Hugh Grant sounds like I hobnob with celebrities all the time, but in fact it was for a magazine article, and remains one of the most exciting days of my life, particularly given that every romantic hero in my early books was based on some version of Hugh Grant. And, readers, he was, indeed, utterly adorable: thoughtful, curious, gossipy, and disarmingly good company.

He also loved my cooking, so he is extra-specially nice and welcome to have lunch in my kitchen. Any. Time. He. Wants.

Now on to more important stuff . . . the food. For those of you who wish to have a taste of my experience with Hugh Grant, I have provided the recipes for the food I made. It was, if I do say so myself, seriously delish.

I had borrowed my friend Wolfie's house in which to cook HG lunch. Once upon a time, it used to belong to Tina Turner, so it's particularly lovely, in Notting Hill, and has La Cornue wall to wall in the kitchen.

Sadly, when I got there, I remembered that Wolfie doesn't cook. I only remembered this an hour before HG arrived, as I went to blend the stuffing and realized the hand-held blender was from 1984 and emitted worrying whiffs of smoke every time I turned it on.

And then—oh the horror—not a sharp knife in the house. I ran over to the hotel up the road, burst in and babbled something about HG coming for lunch and no knives and please, please, please may I borrow their very best carving knife. They said yes.

SERVES 8

### Ingredients:

All-purpose flour, for work surface

1 sheet frozen puff pastry, thawed

½ cup (1 stick) unsalted butter

½ cup packed light-brown sugar

2 pounds (about 9) ripe black plums, halved and pitted

¼ teaspoon fine salt

### Method:

Preheat oven to 400 degrees.

On a lightly floured surface, roll out puff pastry into roughly an 18" circle. Refrigerate for around 1 hour.

Spread butter thickly over a medium-sized skillet, and sprinkle sugar on top. Place plums, cut side up (as in, flat side facing you), in concentric circles in a single layer, with the plums touching.

Place skillet on high heat for a few seconds, then turn down to simmer. The butter and sugar will quickly melt and start to caramelize. Leave on heat for 7–8 minutes.

Remove pan from heat and drape pastry over top, tucking any small overhangs inside the pan around the edges of the outside layer of plums. Bake 30–40 minutes, invert onto plate, and serve with ice cream.

# FLOURLESS CHOCOLATE CHESTNUT TRUFFLE TORTE

This is my favorite chocolate dessert of all time, possibly because it is like a giant slice of chocolate truffle heaven. You don't taste the chestnuts at all, but they give it an extraordinary richness, and it truly is like eating a giant slice of light truffle.

I also love that it's flourless and only has a tiny amount of sugar. If you force yourself to forget about the butter, this could almost be diet food . . .

Almost.

It is ridiculously easy. I made this one morning, and left the house with an entire cake intact. By the time I got back, the Smalls had attacked, and there was less than a quarter left!

With thanks to Hugh Fearnley-Whitingstall for his gorgeous recipe, which has only been changed very, very slightly.

SERVES 8–10

## Ingredients:

1 cup semisweet chocolate chips

1 cup (2 sticks) unsalted butter, cubed

1 cup peeled, cooked chestnuts (I find them in jars or cans)

1 cup half-and-half

6 eggs, separated

½ cup sugar

1 teaspoon vanilla extract

## Method:

Preheat oven to 350 degrees.

Grease and line a 9" springform cake tin.

Melt the chocolate and butter together in a pan over a very gentle heat. In another pan, heat the chestnuts with the milk until just boiling, then mash thoroughly with a potato masher (or process to a rough purée in a machine).

Put the egg yolks in a bowl and mix with the sugar. Stir in the chocolate mixture, vanilla extract and chestnut purée until you have a smooth, blended batter. Whisk the egg whites until stiff and fold them carefully into the batter.

Transfer the mixture to the greased, lined tin and bake for 25–30 minutes, or until the cake is just set, but still has a slight wobble.

If you want to serve the cake warm, leave to cool a little, then release the tin and slice carefully—it will be very soft and moussey. Or leave to cool, when it will have set firm. It's good to serve it with a trickle of double cream, especially when warm, but it is also delicious unadulterated.

# ETON MESS

I realize I have become somewhat Americanized when I start thinking about pies, pies and more pies for desserts during the summer.

Which is all well and good, except I don't very much like pies. I *love* crumbles, but only if there's tons of crumble and not a lot of fruit, and the crumble should be moist and crunchy at the same time, and have oatmeal in it, and ... oh goodness. Getting hungry.

But the one thing I do love is meringue. And Pavlova. Last week, with three barbecues to go to and having offered to make dessert for each, I decided to go back to my roots and make good old Eton Mess.

I'm not sure who brought it back in vogue. It's a dish traditionally served at the annual cricket match between Eton and Winchester, but up until a few years ago, only those who actually came up through the ranks of the highest public schools in England knew about it. All of a sudden, Eton Mess was everywhere. I had never been particularly impressed by the mixing up of whipped cream, meringue and strawberries and hadn't bothered making it.

But faced with making pies last weekend, or the rather easier Eton Mess, I opted for Eton Mess, and I have to tell you, the combination of the three, with some added sugar and pomegranate juice, was almost ridiculously sublime. I'd like to say everyone loved it just as much as I did, but they hardly got a look in. I went back for seconds, thirds, and then I stopped counting. Also, do continuous giant heaping spoonfuls count as thirds? Or eighths? Shall I go on?

I also cheated, because I didn't have time, nor the nerves, to make the meringue. I ran up to Trader Joe's and bought a carton of their vanilla meringue cookies and bashed them up with a meat mallet, which I highly recommend if you're in a bad mood.

And so, it was the easiest dish I have ever made. Here I give you a recipe that uses store-bought meringues because they are the perfect meringues for Eton Mess, and it makes no difference to the finished product, and my meringues are always chewier than this recipe demands. I have added the recipe for the actual meringue, should you be tempted to try the whole thing from scratch.

# ETON MESS

SERVES 6–8

## Ingredients:

4 cups strawberries

2 teaspoons sugar

2 teaspoons pomegranate juice (or purist version: separate 2 cups strawberries from above and purée them in a blender to a juice)

2 cups heavy whipping cream

14–16 individual meringue nests

### Strawberry Coulis:

1 cup strawberries

2 teaspoons sugar

1 teaspoon lemon juice

### Meringues:

3 large egg whites

¾ cup sugar

## Method:

Make strawberry coulis by heating strawberries, sugar and lemon juice until soft and pulpy. Remove from heat and blend. Set aside.

Hull and chop the strawberries quite roughly, place in bowl and add sugar, pomegranate juice and strawberry coulis, reserving ¼ cup strawberry coulis to drizzle over finished mixture. Set aside.

Whip the cream in a large bowl until thick peaks form. DO NOT OVERDO OR YOU'LL HAVE BUTTER. Roughly crumble in 8 of the meringues, large chunks and small.

Fold together with strawberry mixture, drizzling remaining strawberry coulis over top. You can make a large glass bowl or fill pretty individual glasses and garnish individually. Decorate with chopped strawberries and remaining meringues.

### If you are tempted to make the meringues from scratch:

Preheat oven to 300 degrees.

Whisk the egg whites in a cold, clean bowl until you have soft peaks. Add the sugar, VERY SLOWLY SO AS NOT TO ATTRACT MOISTURE, 1 tablespoon at a time, and whisk until all the sugar has been mixed in properly.

Drop dessert spoons of meringue on a baking sheet, place in oven on center shelf, turn the heat down to 275 degrees and leave for 1 hour.

Then turn the oven off, and leave the meringues in the oven to dry out overnight, or at the very least, until the oven is completely cold.

# WHIPPED MAPLE RICOTTA ICE CREAM

We were on Nantucket, and meeting new friends of ours who had turned out to be old friends of Beloved's parents, and who he hadn't seen since, well, birth. We were stuck as to what to bring. Blue hydrangeas just seemed a bit... unnecessary, and they had plenty of wine, so we settled on dessert, a whipped ricotta with berries.

They were renting a house for the summer that was listed for sale. It had been finished about 5 minutes before they moved in and had more bells and whistles than anything I'd ever seen.

They gave us the grand tour, saving the best until last—the basement, which housed a huge movie theater complete with wall-to-wall dioramas of a busy main street, beautifully backlit; a steam room big enough for the Yankees and their friends; and a dedicated massage room.

It was ridiculous, and fantastic, the quintessential fantasy house, a millionaire's playground. And after we got the tour, we trooped upstairs for dinner, ending with this yummy dessert that needs nothing other than a big bowl, a spoon and willing fingers for clean-up when no one is looking.

The only thing that could possibly have made it better would have been to turn it into ice cream, which is exactly what I did the next time I made it.

SERVES 6

### Ingredients:

**4 egg yolks**

**2 tablespoons sugar**

**2 cups whole milk ricotta cheese**

**½ cup cream cheese, softened at room temp**

**3 tablespoons maple syrup**

**1 teaspoon vanilla extract**

### Method:

Whisk egg yolks and sugar together until pale and creamy.

Blend rest of ingredients in a food processor until very smooth (about 5 minutes). Add egg yolks and blend until well combined.

Transfer to glass dish with lid and place in freezer for around 6 hours. Or place in ice cream maker and follow instructions.

# BEST CHOCOLATE CHIP COOKIES

Before I moved to America, I'm not sure I ever really understood the appeal of chocolate chip cookies, nor why they were so ubiquitous over here. Growing up in London the cookies—or as we call them, *biscuits*—I made were shortbread, chocolate cornflake cakes, flapjacks. I don't think I'd ever made a chocolate chip cookie in my life.

My first Christmas here, I was invited to a cookie exchange. I spent hours cooking elaborate chocolate-covered Florentines, arriving to find myself amidst a plethora of varying chocolate chip cookies. I will say my Florentines won best cookie of the night (unofficially, from the husband), but I also discovered just how many variations of chocolate chip cookies there are.

The Neiman Marcus cookies are sinfully amazing—large, chewy, chunky—and you will find the recipe underneath. These cookies are thinner, crispier, more delicate, and I think more sophisticated. Either works!

MAKES 2 DOZEN

### Ingredients:

1 cup (2 sticks) butter

¾ cup brown sugar

¾ cup white sugar

2 eggs, beaten

2 teaspoons vanilla extract

2¼ cups all-purpose flour

1 teaspoon baking soda

1 teaspoon salt

2 cups chocolate chips

### Method:

Preheat oven to 350 degrees.

In a large bowl, cream together butter and brown and white sugars until pale and fluffy. Add eggs, a little at a time, beating well with each addition. Stir in vanilla.

In a separate bowl, combine flour, baking soda and salt. Gradually stir into the creamed mixture. Finally, fold in chocolate chips.

Drop in rounded spoonfuls on greased baking sheets or Silpat-lined cookie trays.

Bake for 8–10 minutes until light brown. Place on wire rack to cool.

# NEIMAN MARCUS CHOCOLATE CHIP COOKIES

There is an undoubtedly apocryphal story that goes with these cookies, of a woman who ate them in the restaurant of the aforementioned store, and the cookies were so extraordinarily amazing (which they are), she asked for the recipe. It was supplied, together with a bill for $250.

Horrified at the price, the story goes, she took the recipe, gave it to everyone she knew and plastered it all over the Internet. The story has been gathering steam for years, although it seems highly improbable. Happily, regardless of how or where the story emerged and whether or not it is true, these cookies truly may be the most magnificent cookies ever created.

They are dense, and thick, and chewy, and oatmealy and chocolatey. Have you ever read a happier sentence in your life?

MAKES 10 DOZEN

## Ingredients:

5 cups blended oatmeal

2 cups (4 sticks) butter

2 cups white sugar

2 cups brown sugar

4 eggs

2 teaspoons vanilla extract

4 cups flour

1 teaspoon salt

2 teaspoons baking powder

2 teaspoons baking soda

4 cups chocolate chips

1 (8-ounce) Hershey Bar, grated

3 cups chopped nuts (your choice)

## Method:

Preheat oven to 375 degrees.

Measure oatmeal and blend in a blender to a fine powder.

Cream the butter and both sugars until pale.

Add eggs and vanilla to the butter and mix.

In a separate bowl, combine flour, oatmeal, salt, baking powder and soda and mix with egg and butter.

Fold in chocolate chips, Hershey Bar and nuts.

Roll into balls and place 2" apart on a cookie sheet or drop by teaspoonful onto the cookie sheet.

Bake for 8–10 minutes. Cool on a wire rack.

# GLUTEN-FREE COCONUT AND CHOCOLATE MACAROONS

Although you might not know it from the recipes contained within, much of my time is spent avoiding sugar and flour. As a result of undiagnosed Lyme disease, I now deal with a host of autoimmune syndromes, and find I do much better when I am avoiding my addictions. My kids, too. In fact, my youngest, at 10 years old, announced one day he wanted to eat the way I was eating. He cut out all sugar, flour and processed foods, and two weeks later, it was as if someone had replaced my child. The boy who I had always called the Maniac was now calm, gentle, sweet. His rage and volatility were all but gone, and he felt so fantastic, he is not only approaching six months, his siblings are doing it, too.

But what child can subsist on protein, vegetables, salads and fruits alone? The cravings do occasionally need to be satisfied, and this is how we do it, with these fail-safe cookies. The kids love them. Sometimes I'll dip the tops in dark chocolate at the end. You would never know that they are spectacularly healthy.

SERVES 6–8

## Ingredients:

2 cups shredded coconut

¼ cup almond flour

⅛ teaspoon sea salt

1 teaspoon Stevia

½ teaspoon baking powder

2 tablespoons coconut oil or unsalted butter, melted

3 eggs, beaten

1 teaspoon vanilla extract

1 teaspoon almond extract

¼ cup maple syrup

¼ cup coconut milk

¼ cup dark chocolate chips

## Method:

Preheat oven to 325 degrees.

Mix together shredded coconut, almond flour, sea salt, Stevia and baking powder.

In a separate bowl, mix coconut oil or butter with beaten eggs, vanilla and almond extracts, maple syrup, and coconut milk.

Mix wet and dry ingredients together. Fold in chocolate chips.

Mound in small pyramid-shaped heaps on an oiled baking sheet, and bake for 18–20 minutes until golden.

Cool on a wire rack.

# GINGER ICE CREAM

I think I may have to replace my ice cream maker. Either that or try to find a new set of instructions. This may be because I am a woman, or possibly because I have, as my husband says, the patience of a fruit fly, but I do not *do* instruction booklets. Ever. I think it may be a genetic malfunction, but if I open an instruction booklet, the words all start to fuzz and move about, and the only thing left to do is set it aside and figure it out myself.

Usually, I do pretty well. But not, it seems, with the ice cream maker. It may also be that I always leave it to the last minute, but my guests are getting very used to warm, soupy ice cream.

However, this ginger ice cream that I made the other day is so fantastic none of them cared. Next time, I'm buying a new ice cream maker, and I shall hand the booklet straight to Beloved so he can tell me how it works.

SERVES 6–8

### Ingredients:

3 cups heavy cream

1 cup whole milk

¼ cup grated fresh ginger

Pinch of salt

½ teaspoon vanilla extract

8 egg yolks

¾ cup sugar

¼ cup finely chopped crystallized ginger (more if, like me, you love it!)

### Method:

In a large, heavy saucepan, combine the cream, milk, fresh ginger, vanilla, and salt over medium heat and simmer for 20 minutes.

Whisk the egg yolks and sugar together until pale gold and fluffy. Add one ladleful of the hot cream mixture into eggs, combine, then add all eggs into hot cream mixture. Stir constantly for around 5 minutes until the custard mixture is thick enough to coat the back of a spoon.

Strain over a fine-meshed sieve into a large bowl, pressing with the back of the spoon to extract as much liquid as you can. Cover tightly and refrigerate until cold—at least 3 hours.

Add the crystallized ginger to the cold cream mixture, then pour into the bowl of an ice cream maker and freeze according to manufacturer's instructions. Transfer the ice cream to an airtight container and freeze until ready to eat.

# CHOCOLATE MOUSSE CAKE

Summer was approaching and one of the Smalls announced they were distinctly unhappy with the prospect of getting into a bathing suit and could we all be a bit healthier please.

There happened to be a birthday coming up, with lots of children coming over, but this particular Small wanted to try to avoid the store-bought, multicolored cake filled with—doubtless—additives, and sugar, and chemicals. I can't say I particularly blamed them, so also on offer was this chocolate mousse cake, flour-free and, in my version, sweetened with Stevia instead of sugar.

All the Smalls, bless them, eschewed the cake that was demolished by their friends and, instead cut huge slices of this dense, chocolatey cake, declaring it the best birthday cake they had ever had. This from 11-year-olds. I had to put it in.

SERVES 6–8

**Ingredients:**

**4 ounces fine-quality bittersweet chocolate (not unsweetened)**

**½ cup (1 stick) unsalted butter**

**4 large eggs, separated**

**¾ teaspoon Stevia (or ¾ cup sugar)**

**½ cup unsweetened cocoa powder plus additional for sprinkling**

**Ganache:**

**1 cup semisweet chocolate chips**

**1 cup heavy cream**

**Method:**

Preheat oven to 375 degrees.

Butter an 8" round baking pan. Line bottom with a round of wax paper and butter paper.

Melt chocolate with butter, stirring until smooth.

Combine egg yolks and Stevia, whisk well. Add to chocolate mixture.

Beat egg whites until stiff.

Fold 1 spoon of chocolate mix into egg whites, then fold rest of whites into chocolate until well combined.

Pour batter into pan and bake in middle of oven for 25 minutes, or until top has formed a thin crust. Cool and invert onto plate.

Either dust cake with additional cocoa powder or make a ganache: melt chocolate chips with cream until smooth, spread over top and sides, and cool in fridge.

# SCONES

What self-respecting Englishwoman would write a cookbook and not have a recipe for scones?

No English tea is complete without cucumber sandwiches and scones with clotted cream and jam. Some of my favorite childhood memories involve going to my Great Auntie Lena's house for tea. She had tiny bridge rolls with egg salad, cucumber sandwiches, wonderful petit fours and scones. She also had a cat who was terrified of us, which didn't stop my brother and me from desperately trying to entice it out from under the bed to cuddle it.

When I first moved to this country, I regularly threw tea parties, leaving my friends and neighbors slightly bewildered, but happy. They were excellent at the impromptu barbeque, but no one did teas better than me.

I am still slightly unclear as to whether it is jam first, then cream, or the other way round. And I understand it hinges on whether you are serving tea in Devon or Cornwall. I tend to slather on the jam, then add a large dollop of the cream.

You can fancy the scones up by adding raisins, sultanas or even chocolate chips, but frankly I prefer them utterly plain. A couple of tips—work the dough only until it all holds together, no more than absolutely necessary to keep the scones light, and cut with a 2" wide fluted round pastry cutter. These are British scones, slightly bigger than bite-size and definitely not the large, triangular versions we see in America.

# SCONES

SERVES 6–8

## Ingredients:

3 cups all-purpose flour

2½ tablespoons baking powder

¼ teaspoon salt

2 tablespoons sugar

1¼ cups plain Greek yogurt

4¼ tablespoons milk

⅓ cup melted butter

1 egg to wash pastry

## Method:

Preheat oven to 425 degrees.

Sift together flour, baking powder and salt. Add sugar.

In a separate bowl, whisk together yogurt and milk until well combined, then add melted butter. Combine with the flour mix in a large bowl.

Bring the dough together by kneading and turning in the bowl until all the dough is sticking together, pressing down until all the floury bits at the bottom of the bowl have been gathered into the dough.

Turn onto a floured surface and knead a couple of times, then roll out to a thickness of about ¾".

Using the pastry cutter, cut the scones out and place them, touching each other, on a Silpat-lined baking tray.

Whisk egg and brush surface of scones with egg.

Bake for 12–14 minutes, or until golden brown.

Allow to cool before piling with jam and clotted cream.

# GUILT-FREE CHOCOLATE NUT TRUFFLES

If you are on a healthy path, or even considering it, these make great after-school treats and are equally good after dinner parties. They are not too sweet and deliciously dense. They have been my favorite after-dinner treat for the past three years.

SERVES 6

### Ingredients:

1 cup nuts (cashews, macadamia or almonds)

3–4 tablespoons raw cacao powder

1 teaspoon vanilla extract

2 tablespoons agave nectar

2 tablespoons coconut oil

Unsweetened cocoa powder or shredded coconut to finish

### Method:

Grind nuts and cacao in a blender until smooth. Add vanilla, agave necter and coconut oil and process until blended.

Form into balls, around 1", and roll in cocoa powder or coconut shreds to finish.

Refrigerate for at least 1 hour before serving.

With love,

June x.

# THANK YOU

A huge thank-you to the people who were so instrumental in bringing this book to life and helping spread the good word.

For giving me the idea in the first place, Edward Ash-Milby; for bringing it to fruition, Christy Fletcher, Sylvie Greenberg, and Hillary Black at Fletcher & Co, and Alex Daly, Sarah Meister and Kriti Upadhyay at Vann Alexander; for the gorgeous photography, Tom McGovern and Kyran Tompkins; for cooking up a delicious storm, Nicole Straight and Keith Jacob; for keeping our kitchen beautifully organized, Valerie Bensch and Diane Sousa; for the gorgeous props and support, Kim, Alison and Wende Cohen at Bungalow, Sarah Kaplan at Dovecote and Terry Storz; for the spectacular design and art direction, Carol Buettner and Russ Hardin; for the brilliant shout-outs, Emily Giffin, Amanda Hesser, Jen Lancaster, Lisa Lampanelli, Jodi Picoult, Martha Stewart, Lee Woodruff and so many others. And of course to my most beloved family, Ian, Max, Harry, Tabitha, Nate and Jasper, for being such willing guinea pigs for so long. And to my mum, without whom there would have been no love of food, feeding people and knowing how to cook your way to people's hearts.

A huge thank-you to these incredible backers for their extraordinary support: Stacy Bass, John Belfatto, Sheri Biller, Brent Rice, Daniel De Rocco, Mette Feldt, Jaclyn Goldis, Robin Homonoff, Steven March, Tessa Smith McGovern, Julie Meister, Clea Newman, Riann Smith, Hilary Trader, Julian Vogel, Ian Warburg, Jeff Warshaw and Steve T. Zelson.

# ACKNOWLEDGMENTS

And another thank-you for so much kindness and support:

Shauna Abbrederis and Kristen Abbrederis, Kathryn Allen, Jamie Anderson, Amy Ballard, Tonia Barringer, Jessica Bell, Janet Bellows, Erin Berk, Sophie Cabot Black, Ruma Bose, Marie Bostwick, Jacqueline Byrne, Lissa Chesnoff, Norma Christensen, Noelle Christie, Sue Clarke, Cathy Cole, Leann Combis, Sarah Day, Katie Devine, Helen Dewar, Cristina Dolan, Betty Doyle, Tracy Dubin, Alyson Durand, Dian Dutro, Elizabeth Colbert, Karen Siff Exkorn, Robyn Feldberg, Rebecca Feldman, Juanita Ferrante, Sarah Fielden, Sandi Haber Fifield, Alan and Laraine Fischer, Christy Fletcher, Sandra Fossum, Michelle Friedman, Pamela C. Gamble, Fiona Garland and Andy Bentley, Shani Raine Gilchrist, Sharon Gitelle, Marnie Goldman, Bruce and Robbie Green, Charlie and Karen Green, Ann Grismore, Kristin Lowe Hale, Sarah Hall, Diane Russom Harrison, Amy Hatvany, Sterling Hawkins, Marisol Herrera, Katherine Daught Jacob, Mindy Jason, Pamela Johnson, Jeffrey Jones, Keith and Cari Kaplan, Bonnie Zobel Karoly, Amiram Katz, Julie J. Kenney, Ranjiv Khush, Katura Klaus, Jennifer Lancaster, Brian and Tasha Lansbury, Kerry Gallagher Ledbetter, Michelle Leininger, Andrea Leung, Wende Cohen and Rick Levin, Zorba and Kristi Lieberman, Katie Luebke, Caroline MacDougall, Michael Maren and Dani Shapiro, Sashia McCosker, Jen McCoy, Sarah McCoy, Vickie Ann McCoy, Barbara McKechnie, Carrie Medders, Sarah Meister, Emily Miller, Ron Nash, John Nugent and Elle Fure, Julie Barrett O'Brien, Mary O'Connor, Joy Pavelchak, Jenn Penn, Jamie Petrilli, Ann Pisetzner, Sophie and Stefan Pollmann, Kate Poznan, Joshlyn Racherbaumer, Linus Raines, Jim Randel, Abbie Rawlings-Green and Jonny Lach, Tracey Reid, Maria Retartha, Eric Ries, Mary Beth Roche, Sarah Rocketto, Aini Rockwell, Aidan Donnelley Rowley, Michael Runyon, Susanna Sachau, Erika Sales, Jeffrey and Carolyn Salzman, Katie Sawicki, Carly Schofield, Sheila Schwartz, Joanna Herbst Scott, Robin Selden, Danielle Sharp, Erika Sherry, Violeta Srdanovic, Elizabeth Steffen, Helen Sturm, Colleen Sullivan, April Ure, Erin L. Verespy, Amy Vischio, Sam Walker, Wendy Walker, Natalia and David Warburg, Joan Warren, Amy Waters, Julie Whamond, Anne Whelton, Kristen Wilkinson, Courtney Williams, Jeanne Wisniewski, Amy Withers, Stephanie Yeo and Randall Zuckerman.

# INDEX OF RECIPES

# ENDINGS

# ABOUT JANE

Jane Green is the author of seventeen novels, including sixteen *New York Times* bestsellers.

A native Londoner, she is published in over twenty-five languages and has over 10 million books in print worldwide. A former journalist in the UK, she is also a regular contributor to radio and television including morning shows such as *Good Morning America* and the *Today Show*.

Together with writing books and blogs, she contributes to various publications, both online and print, including anthologies and novellas, and features for the *Huffington Post*, the *Sunday Times*, *Cosmopolitan* and *Self*. She has taught at writers' conferences and does regular keynote speaking.

A graduate of the International Culinary Center in New York, Jane filled two of her books, *Saving Grace* and *Promises to Keep*, with recipes culled from her own collection. She says she only cooks food that is "incredibly easy, but has to look as if you have slaved over a hot stove for hours." This is because she has five children and has realized that "when you have five children, nobody ever invites you anywhere."

Jane lives in Westport, Connecticut, with her husband and their blended family. When she is not writing, cooking, gardening, decorating, filling her house with friends and herding chickens, she is usually sleeping.

Vist Jane online at janegreen.com; facebook.com/authorjanegreen; and instagram.com/janegreen.author.

A HOUSE IS MADE OF WOOD AND STONE,
　　　BUT HOMES ARE MADE OF LOVE ALONE.

Anonymous